Great Year-Round

GRILLING

in the

MIDWEST

Great Year-Round
GRILLING
in the
MIDWEST

The Flavors • The Culinary Traditions • The Techniques

Ellen Brown

The Lyons Press
Guilford, Connecticut
An imprint of The Globe Pequot Press

The Lyons Press is an imprint of The Globe Pequot Press

Photos on the following pages courtesy of Shutterstock: xiii, 1, 3, 8, 9, 14, 16, 18, 22, 23, 28, 36, 51, 57, 59, 68, 73, 74, 82, 87, 92, 95, 101, 104, 118

Photos on the following pages courtesy of Jupiterimages: xii, 2, 5, 32, 37, 38, 42, 46, 49, 52, 61, 67, 75, 96, 98, 103, 111, 114, 116, 120, 121

Photo of engraving on page xi courtesy of the Library of Congress

Photo on page 94 courtesy of Photos.com

Text design by Sheryl P. Kober

Library of Congress Cataloging-in-Publication Data
Brown, Ellen.
  Great year-round grilling in the Midwest : the flavors—the culinary traditions—the techniques / Ellen Brown.
    p. cm.
  ISBN 978-1-59921-481-8
  1. Barbecue cookery—Middle West. 2. Cookery, American—Midwestern style. I. Title.
  TX840.B3B75783 2009
  641.7'60977—dc22

Printed in China

10 9 8 7 6 5 4 3 2 1

This book is dedicated, with my love, to Marilyn and Sam Krimm, who have been grilling in Ann Arbor, Michigan, for most of my life and introduced me to Paris and its food.

Contents

This chapter includes everything you need to know about grills and grilling to successfully cook all the recipes in the book, beginning with the principles of grilling; charcoal vs. gas grills; accessories for ease and safety; grilling safety; how to gauge when the grill is ready to cook; how to use wood chips to add smoky flavor to foods; and how to create multi-level fires.

There are four basic ways to flavor food before it goes on the grill—rubs, pastes, marinades, and brines—and the amount of time required to impart flavor ranges from seconds to days. Some encompass cooking from various regions of America, as well as cuisines from around the world.

This chapter includes sauces to dress up grilled food and elevate a simple entree to a dish of distinction. These sauces are versatile, and can go with many types of food; each recipe is annotated with the categories of grilled food for which it is compatible.

Grilled hors d'oeuvres are as varied as slices of toasted bruschetta topped with fresh tomatoes to Thai chicken satay with peanut sauce. What differentiates hors d'oeuvres from appetizers is that the former are "finger food" and can be eaten without a plate and fork.

From Grilled Corn Soup to Farmer's Market Vegetable Soup, grilling adds its flavor to the main ingredients that go into soups, and in the same way small salads can be topped with grilled fare or include grilled ingredients. The salads in this chapter are small appetizers rather than the larger entree salads of Chapter 11.

While the states of the Midwest are landlocked, there is a wealth of aquatic species caught in the Great Lakes. The recipes in this chapter highlight such fish as walleye pike and rainbow trout, as well as fish caught in waters around the world.

Contents

Contents

Thin-crust pizzas cooked on the grill can be topped with myriad ingredients, some with meats and others with vegetables. The chapter includes a foolproof recipe for basic pizza dough, with various recipes for topping it.

If a grill is lit, it seems senseless to use another cooking method for complementary components of the meal. Grilled vegetables are as varied as kebabs of peppers and onion and heads of radicchio to that greatest of all summer treats—farm-fresh corn. Many of the recipes can also be served as vegetarian entrees.

While there are recipes for vegetable and other side dishes in this book that are cooked on the grill, there are many times that the grill is reserved for the entree, and the supporting players are created in the kitchen. Corn in all forms remains important in the Midwest region. Many side dishes we consider "all American," such as macaroni and cheese and deviled eggs, began there.

The title of this chapter is not an oxymoron, nor is it just variations on toasted marshmallows—although a recipe for S'mores is included. The grill is a natural way to glean the most luscious flavor from fruit because heating enhances all of fruit's natural sweetness as well as creating a softer texture; fruit desserts comprise the majority of these recipes.

The sorts of homey pies and cakes that one finds judged at state fairs are the most typical Midwestern desserts; in this chapter you will find many examples of these made with a variety of native fruits. Interspersed are recipes for dishes that are national favorites—from Strawberry Shortcake to cookies.

Preface

To me, grilling is more than a way of cooking; it's a way of life. The process of grilling food arouses so many sensual pleasures that the end result is more than just a meal. Perhaps that is the reason why I grill year-round; the aroma of food cooking on the grill is as welcome when bundled up against the January cold as it is when lounging in the balmy breezes of July.

Grilling is hardly an exact science; every fire, even one ignited on a gas grill, is different, just as every piece of food cooked on it is unique. The temperature of the air, the velocity and direction of the wind, and the relative humidity all have to be factored into how long it will take a grill to heat and how long it will take food to cook on it. That means that your eyes play a major role when grilling to judge what "done" means, as you poke at food to judge its texture. The sound of food searing adds aural expectation to the experience, and then there's the aroma—emerging not just from the grill but also from the food itself as the steam rises from the plate and reaches the nose.

Grilling, more than any other cooking method, provides an opportunity to share the process with those who will benefit from the results. While a few friends might keep me company in the kitchen from time to time, conventional cooking is basically a solitary endeavor. But a grill becomes the center of a social event, and hovering around it while chatting or sipping is anticipation of a meal that both the cook and the guests can enjoy. Grilling is part of Americans' way of life, be it limited to the summer months in some states and year-round in others.

For the past twenty-five years my personal grilling has taken place in the Northeast. I currently live in Rhode Island, but I've grilled on beaches and decks on Nantucket, and lit many grills in brick-floored Georgetown courtyards while living in Washington. But my first grill was a hibachi on a tiny deck in Cincinnati, Ohio, where I entered the newspaper business in the early 1970s. It was in Cincinnati, and later across the Ohio River in Covington, Kentucky, that I cut my eye-teeth on all aspects of cooking—including grilling.

While living there I also took weekend "field trips" to wonderful farming communities in rural Indiana as well as to cosmopolitan centers like Chicago and St. Louis. From these visits I grew to appreciate the straightforward honesty of Midwestern life and cooking. The roots of Midwestern cooking date back to the late eighteenth century; Germanic and Scandinavian immigrants planted culinary concepts as well as crops along with those of the English settlers.

But this early culinary history has been tempered by the waves of immigrants who arrived from the nineteenth to twenty-first centuries, and as the size and scope of our larder is increasing exponentially with air travel and modern agricultural practices. That is why there are so many international dishes along with traditional American foods in this book; it is those foods that reflect the America of today and the various ethnic heritages that are now blended into those of the original settlers.

I hope you enjoy grilling the dishes in this book, and I hope that as you grill them you allow the pleasures of grilling to become a larger part of your life.

—Ellen Brown
Providence, Rhode Island

While writing a book is a solitary endeavor, its publication is always a team effort. My thanks go to:

Eugene Brissie of The Lyons Press for envisioning such an exciting project.

Ed Claflin, my agent, for his constant support and great humor.

The talented staff at Lyons Press, especially to Ellen Urban for her knowledgeable editorial guidance, Diana Nuhn for the crash course she provided on photo selection, Sheryl Kober for her inspired design, and Jessie Shiers for her eagle-eyed editing.

Constance Brown and Kenn Speiser, my dear neighbors and friends, who good-heartedly ignored the constant smoke from my grills wafting into their backyard from mine.

My many friends whose palates and culinary savvy aided me in recipe development, most especially my beloved sister, Nancy Dubler.

Tigger and Patches, my furry companions, who personally endorse all fish and seafood dishes.

The History of Food Traditions in the Midwestern States

Cooking in the heartland is cooking from the heart. There is a generosity of spirit that goes along with the simple, hearty dishes drawn from the diverse ethnic cuisines brought to the Midwestern states. These settlers, who joined what were then Americans moving from states in the original thirteen colonies, were primarily northern European immigrants in the nineteenth century; they were joined by an ever more diverse group of national enclaves in the twentieth century.

The land east of the Mississippi River was acquired from the British as part of the Treaty of Paris in 1783, and was designated as the Northwest Territory. What we now know as Ohio was settled by veterans of the Revolutionary War who were given land grants by the government; many of the original settlers of Indiana and Illinois moved there from the Carolinas and Virginia, and brought what had become their Southern food traditions with them, including cole slaw and buttermilk biscuits.

The land west of the Mississippi River became part of the country in 1803 as part of the Louisiana Purchase. Although it was purchased from the French, there is little—if any—French culinary influence. The French had virtually ignored the region and it remained the domain of the Native Americans, although some of the first settlers of Michigan came from the French sections of Canada.

The first Homestead Act, passed by Congress in 1862, enabled the head of a family to claim 160 acres in Kansas for only a small filing fee and a commitment to remain on the land for five years. These Homestead Acts continued to be revised as new land was opened up in North and South Dakota, Iowa, and Nebraska. These lands attracted new groups of immigrants, including Poles, Irish, Czechs, and Austrians.

But the region was hardly empty; there was a flourishing Native American civilization. The Ojibway, Ottawa, and Potawatomi tribes of Native Americans

Corn, growing in the wide open spaces in Midwestern states, became a staple of American cuisine.

State fairs have been an important part of life in the Midwest since the nineteenth century.

greeted the European settlers in the Great Lakes region. While they grew the same corn, squash, and beans as Native Americans in other regions, the growing season was so short that they also relied on nuts and seeds for survival.

The Sioux and Chippewa tribes introduced the Europeans to a prized Midwestern crop—wild rice. This aquatic grass native to the northern parts of Michigan, Wisconsin, and Minnesota has to be harvested by hand from shallow waters, a labor-intensive task even today.

While the region is known for its plains and grasslands that support everything from massive amounts of corn to apples, wheat, and potatoes, there are also hilly areas in the northern tier of the states, and many fish are caught in the fresh waters of the Great Lakes and inland streams that feed them. Johnny Appleseed made it as far west as Illinois, planting trees before his death in 1805, and the settlers from other states brought the seeds of peach, cherry, and plum trees with them.

Dairy is central to Midwestern cooking, including eggs, butter, and cheese. Wisconsin produces more cheese than any other state in the country, and Indiana is its leading egg producer. In 1844 a terrible crop failure occurred in Switzerland, and in response the government subsidized emigration of some of the country's farmers to Wisconsin. Experienced in breeding livestock as well as farming, the Swiss settlers built their dairy herds, and by the 1860s cheese-making had progressed from a cottage industry to a real industry. Even today there is one dairy cow for every two people living in the state.

This sense of bringing the best from their home countries to augment their new land is a leitmotif of settlement in the Midwest. When the Mennonites from Russia arrived in Kansas in the 1870s, they found farmers in great distress because they relied on spring wheat. However, these immigrants had brought with them the seeds of wheat species that flourished on the steppes of Russia. They planted them and shared them with neighbors, and so growing wheat became viable.

In general, the primary groups who settled in the Midwest during the nineteenth century came from similar climates. Immigrants from Norway, Sweden, Germany, and Holland arrived during the first part of the century, and they were joined by waves of immigration from Poland, Lithuania, and Russia later in the century.

That is the reason why seasoning and spicing is generally mild in the Midwest, and limited to herbs used fresh from the garden in summer and dried in winter. The Scandinavian settlers brought dill, which was then planted alongside the sage, thyme, and parsley brought from other parts of Europe. Spices such as cinnamon, nutmeg, and allspice play a minor role in the food; however, it is only in the past century that Mediterranean flavors such as oregano and basil have joined the panoply of seasonings.

The large number of German immigrants brought with them the tradition of beer-making, which continues to flourish in the Midwest; it used the grains grown in the region and then the finished product was shipped around the country. And along with the beer were myriad sausages and wurst of all shapes and sizes, many of which are excellent when cooked on a grill.

Chapter 1

Grilling Fundamentals

The unifying factor to most of the recipes in this book—excluding many desserts and side dishes—is that at some point food comes into contact with a grill. This chapter introduces you to the basic equipment and techniques used when grilling food.

Charcoal Grills

All charcoal grills have two grates; the lower grate holds the charcoal and the upper grate holds the food. Charcoal briquettes or hardwood charcoal rest on the lower grate, and once they are lit you can move them around to create the heat pattern that is best for each recipe.

The temperature of the fire is controlled by opening and closing the top and bottom vents. The more these vents are open, the hotter the fire will be, and the more they are closed, the cooler the fire.

Charcoal briquettes are the fuel used overwhelmingly by charcoal grillers, accounting for almost 90 percent of the charcoal purchased in 2007. Invented by automotive pioneer Henry Ford, briquettes are made of low-quality, powdered charcoal and binders that are compressed and molded into little black pillows.

An alternative to briquettes is hardwood charcoal, created by burning hardwood in a furnace using very little oxygen. A piece of hardwood charcoal is

Unlike conventional cooking, grills can be set up anywhere—including on the shores of secluded lakes.

One of the great twentieth-century innovations was the covered kettle grill.

• **Self-starting charcoal briquettes.** These are briquettes that are pre-soaked so only lighting is necessary. My suggestion is to start with ten to twelve pre-soaked briquettes, and once they are flaming add conventional charcoal on top. Your food is less likely to develop the petroleum taste associated with lighter fluid.

• **Chimney charcoal lighter.** These are becoming increasingly popular because they do not involve petroleum, but they are a problem to take along for a cookout away from the house because of their bulky size. They are essentially a metal tube with a handle on one side. Inside is a grate to hold the charcoal and a chamber underneath for crumpled newspaper. Light the newspaper using a match or lighter, and set the chimney on the grill grate. The chimney effect takes the newspaper's flames up through the charcoal and lights it. When a white ash forms on the charcoal, pour the lighted coals out onto the charcoal grate.

almost pure carbon, and has neither glue nor additives present. While almost double the cost of generic briquettes, it does burn hotter and the fire can be controlled more effectively than using briquettes.

Starting a charcoal fire is hardly difficult, and depending on how many accouterments you want to buy, you can accomplish the job with very little effort. Here is a summary of the primary ways charcoal fires are lighted:

• **Lighter fluid.** This petroleum product is very volatile, and should be used with extreme caution. Arrange charcoal in a pyramid in the center of your grill, and spray the coals evenly with the fluid until saturated. Allow the liquid to penetrate for 1 minute, and then light the coals in locations all around the base of the pyramid with a long match or a long-handled butane lighter. *Never use additional lighter fluid once the coals have been initially lit and are smoldering.*

Charcoal briquettes are stacked up in a chimney starter, with newspaper stuffed into the bottom chamber for fuel.

Tips for All Charcoal Grills

While charcoal grills range from small ones designed for picnics to ones encased in extravagant outdoor kitchens, certain rules apply. The key to success when grilling over charcoal is how well the fire is built, and then how well it is maintained if grilling for a long duration. Here are some of considerations for all charcoal fires:

- **Use enough charcoal.** This is perhaps the most common foible of charcoal grilling, regardless if the food to be grilled is a lowly hot dog or a luxurious tenderloin of beef. Make sure the fire is 4 inches larger in diameter than the food to be cooked over it. The higher the charcoal is banked, the hotter the fire will be. If you want to cook over a very hot fire, build the coals to within 3 inches of the grate on which the food will cook. Determine the amount of charcoal you need by piling it up under the cooking grate, and then push it into a pyramid for easy lighting or place it in a chimney.

- **Make sure the charcoal is ready.** Whether using briquettes or hardwood charcoal, the visual sign is that all pieces are lightly covered with gray ash. This means that the charcoal is fully lit and hot.

- **Clean out the ashes regularly.** The heat of a charcoal fire can be diminished if the bottom vents are clogged with ashes. Remove both grates, close the bottom vents, and scoop out the ashes. Remember to open the vents before lighting the next batch of charcoal.

- **Close down the grill after cooking.** There is no reason to waste charcoal, so close the top and bottom vents on the grill to shut it off. The half-used charcoal can be placed off to the side and used to refresh the next fire.

Gas Grills

There is no question that a gas grill is more convenient than cooking with charcoal. Lighting a gas grill is like lighting the oven broiler, and gas grills offer

Gas grills are becoming increasingly popular due to the convenience of merely turning on a burner.

unparalleled convenience. Many people believe, however, that what is lost is some of the flavor and aroma transferred to food when cooking on a charcoal grill.

Gas grills use natural or LP gas for heat and flames, so the fire is efficient. Here is how to light most of them, although you should always consult the manufacturer's instructions: Open the cover, and then open the valve of the gas tank. One at a time, turn the controls to high and ignite the corresponding burner with either a long butane lighter, a long match, or the burner's own electronic ignition. Close the cover and wait 15 to 20 minutes for your grill to reach its highest heat.

Stopping a gas grill is just as easy as lighting one. Turn off each burner, and close off the gas valve. Then turn one of the burners on high for 15 seconds to bleed any gas remaining in the line, turn that burner off, and close the cover.

Tips for All Gas Grills

Gas grills are convenient, but there are also some innate safety problems because you are cooking with a highly volatile liquid. Here are some considerations for safety as well as achieving the best flavor:

3

- **Always keep the lid down except if expressly told to leave it open in a recipe.** Gas burns cleanly, so no residue accumulates on the interior of the lid from high-heat cooking.

- **Remove the warming rack, assuming the grill has one, before lighting the grill.** Unless you plan to actually use it, the warming rack gets in the way of turning food at the back of the grate, and can burn your hand as you try.

- **Do not skimp on the preheating time.** It is easy to know when a charcoal fire is ready for cooking, and with a gas grill your only clue is how long it has been heating. Give it a full 15 minutes, and longer in cold weather.

- **Store propane tanks—full or empty—in a well-ventilated space.** They should never be placed in a garage or basement.

Grilling Accessories

Gourmet shops and Web sites are filled with grilling accessories, but there are only a few that are really necessary. Here is a brief list of ones I find useful:

- **Spray bottle.** For problems to be serious enough that a fire extinguisher is necessary is not common; however, minor flare-ups caused by fat dripping onto either charcoal or metal bars are a routine occurrence when grilling. A spray bottle—either purchased for the grill or a well-washed-out one from a cleaning product—is important to keep around at all times. You can target the flames without disturbing the food above them.

- **Stainless-steel tongs.** You should have a few pairs of tongs, with handles at least 12 inches long. Use tongs and not a meat fork for turning food (a meat fork causes food to lose juice and become dry).

- **Spatula.** A long-handled spatula makes flipping hamburgers and moving other foods easy.

- **Grill brush.** Use a grill brush to clean the grate on which the food sits. I clean it once at the end of grilling, and then again before adding food the next time.

- **Instant-read thermometer.** This piece of inexpensive equipment should be mandatory in every kitchen, not only for grilling but for roasting as well. All you have to do is stick it into the thickest part of food and leave it in for 20 seconds, and it registers an accurate reading on the doneness of your food.

- **Metal and bamboo skewers.** While metal skewers are indestructible, they are not as aesthetically pleasing as delicate ones made from bamboo.

Using Wood Chips for Flavor

Wood chips made from aromatic woods like hickory, mesquite, apple, and cherry add immeasurably to the flavor of grilled foods, as well as giving the skin of poultry a rich mahogany color. For charcoal grills, the secret is to soak the chips in water to cover for at least 30 minutes. Even though it is not as pronounced a flavor, you can also use wood chips on a gas grill. Place about 2 cups dry wood chips in the center of a large (12 x 18 inch) piece of heavy-duty aluminum foil. Bring up the foil on all sides and roll the ends together to seal the pouch. Poke several small holes in the top of the packet. Once the grill is hot, place the wood chip pouch under the grate across the burner shields. Smoke will eventually emerge from the holes.

Fire Configurations for Grilling

Each recipe in this book contains information about the appropriate temperature and configuration of the grill for the success of the recipe. This section guides you through what each of these mean.

- **Direct grilling.** This was how all grilling was accomplished prior to the invention of the covered kettle grill and the gas grill. The coals are lit and then evenly spread three to four layers deep on the lower grate.

Long handles are the primary requirement for cooking tools used at the grill.

- **Dual-temperature grilling.** Once the coals are ignited and have reached the desired temperature, you can customize the fire to the needs of the food. By spreading the coals so that they are three or four deep on one side of the grill and one or two layers deep on the other side, you can sear food and then transfer it to the cooler side to complete the cooking. For a gas grill, preheat the grill on high, and then reduce half the burners to medium.

- **Indirect grilling.** When you are cooking by indirect heat on a charcoal grill, what you are actually doing is turning your covered grill into an outdoor oven. The coals are pushed to the periphery of the grill and the food is place in the center over an aluminum drip pan rather than over direct heat. The grill is always kept covered, and the top and bottom vents are partially closed. If you have a gas grill with more than one burner, it is possible to cook over indirect heat. The grills best suited to indirect cooking are those with right and left rather than front and back burners.

Determining the Temperature of a Grill

After the coals have a light coating of ash or the gas burners have been preheated, place your hand, palm-side down, about 4–5 inches above the cooking rack, and count slowly. Here are your readings to determine the temperature of the grill:

- Hot grill: 2 seconds

- Medium-hot grill: 3–4 seconds

- Medium grill: 5–6 seconds

- Medium-low grill: 7 seconds

Grilling is a high-heat cooking method, so if you can hold your hand over the coals for more than 7 seconds, it means you should be adding more coals or preheating the gas burners longer.

Preparing the Grill Grate

Once the grill grate has heated from the fire, take a stiff wire grill brush and brush it well to remove any cooked-on food remaining.

Treating the grid with oil just prior to grilling helps ensure that food will not stick. The best way to do this is to dip a paper towel in vegetable oil, and then, holding it with tongs, rub it all over the grill grate. This is an important step to good grilling.

The Timing of Recipes and How to Use This Book

There is no universal style of cookbook and recipe writing; each author approaches the task in a somewhat personal way. In order to provide you with the maximum number of recipes, the preparation of the fire refers you back to this chapter rather than using space to restate it constantly.

Each recipe is annotated with the number of servings, which is usually given as a range. If the dish is part of a multi-course meal, it can be "stretched" to feed more people; if it is an item that is one-per-person, the number of servings is finite.

"Active time," the second annotation, is the amount of hands-on prep time needed in the kitchen before food goes to the grill. In almost all cases the amount is less than 25 minutes, or less than the amount of time needed for a charcoal grill to heat properly. This is the time measurement for all the chopping, dicing, and indoor cooking.

The third annotation is "Start to finish." While grilling is a cooking method that can be considered "fast food" because it cooks with high heat, the time needed to properly light and heat the grill must always be factored into the equation; it may take only 5 minutes to cook a pounded chicken breast, but that is after the grill is ready to accomplish the task.

The recipes in this book are calculated to factor in the fire preparation as part of the time necessary to complete the dish, and to be on the safe side, the assumption is 25–30 minutes.

Chapter 2

Ways to Flavor Food— Rubs, Pastes, Marinades, and Brines

There are four basic ways to flavor food before it goes on the grill—rubs, pastes, marinades, and brines—and the amount of time required to impart flavor ranges from seconds to days. In this chapter you will find recipes and techniques for all these ways to treat food destined for the grill.

Rubs

Rubs are a relatively new addition to the arsenal of ways to flavor foods, and they truly do offer flavor without fuss. Most rubs are highly concentrated mixtures of herbs and spices that should be applied to food after it has been brushed with oil. And "rub" is what you should do. Rather than just giving food a light sprinkle, rub the mixture into the food with your fingertips.

Asian Five-Spice Rub

Yield: ½ cup | Active time: 5 minutes | Start to finish: 5 minutes | Uses: Meats, poultry, fish and seafood

Combine five-spice powder, brown sugar, garlic powder, and cayenne in a bowl, and mix well. Store in an airtight container in a cool, dry place for up to 1 month.

3 tablespoons Chinese five-spice powder *

2 tablespoons firmly packed light brown sugar

1 teaspoon garlic powder

Cayenne to taste

* Available in the Asian aisle of most supermarkets and in specialty markets.

Creole Rub

Yield: ½ cup | Active time: 5 minutes | Start to finish: 5 minutes | Uses: All foods

Combine paprika, garlic powder, onion powder, oregano, thyme, pepper, and cayenne in a bowl, and mix well. Store in an airtight container in a cool, dry place for up to 1 month.

3 tablespoons paprika

2 tablespoons garlic powder

1 tablespoon onion powder

1 tablespoon dried oregano

1 tablespoon dried thyme

2 teaspoons freshly ground black pepper

1 teaspoon cayenne

Spices such as peppercorns and fennel seeds, should be crushed with a mortar and pestle to release their flavor.

2 tablespoons chili powder

2 tablespoons paprika

1 tablespoon ground cumin

1 tablespoon ground coriander

1 tablespoon garlic powder

1 tablespoon dried oregano

1 teaspoon freshly ground black pepper

1 teaspoon crushed red pepper flakes

South of the Border Rub

Yield: ½ cup | Active time: 5 minutes | Start to finish: 5 minutes | Uses: All foods

Combine chili powder, paprika, cumin, coriander, garlic powder, oregano, black pepper, and red pepper in a bowl, and mix well. Store in an air-tight container in a cool, dry place for up to 1 month.

3 tablespoons dry mustard

2 tablespoon garlic powder

2 tablespoons coarsely ground black pepper

1 tablespoon dried oregano

2 teaspoons dried basil

Steakhouse-Style Rub

Yield: ½ cup | Active time: 5 minutes | Start to finish: 5 minutes | Uses: Beef, lamb

Combine mustard, garlic powder, pepper, oregano, and basil in a bowl, and mix well. Store in an air-tight container in a cool, dry place for up to 1 month.

Spanish Spice Rub

Yield: ½ cup | Active time: 5 minutes | Start to finish: 5 minutes | Uses: All foods

Combine paprika, cumin, mustard, turmeric, and oregano in a bowl, and mix well. Store in an air-tight container in a cool, dry place for up to 1 month.

6 tablespoons smoked Spanish paprika

2 tablespoons ground cumin

1 tablespoon dry mustard

1 tablespoon ground turmeric

1 tablespoon dried oregano

Aromatic Herb and Spice Rub

Yield: ½ cup | Active time: 5 minutes | Start to finish: 5 minutes | Uses: All foods

Combine coriander, thyme, cumin, pepper, oregano, and sage in a bowl, and mix well. Store in an air-tight container in a cool, dry place for up to 1 month.

2 tablespoons ground coriander

2 tablespoons dried thyme

1 tablespoon ground cumin

1 tablespoon freshly ground black pepper

1 tablespoon dried oregano

1 tablespoon dried sage

Basic Herb Rub

Yield: ½ cup | Active time: 5 minutes | Start to finish: 5 minutes | Uses: All foods

Combine rosemary, thyme, sage, tarragon, and pepper in a bowl, and mix well. Store in an air-tight container in a cool, dry place for up to 1 month.

3 tablespoons crumbled dried rosemary

3 tablespoons dried thyme

3 tablespoons dried sage

1 tablespoon dried tarragon

1 tablespoon freshly ground black pepper

To preserve both color and potentcy, spices should be kept in a cool, dry, dark, place.

Pastes

Pastes represent the middle ground between rubs and marinades, and the amount of time needed to use them is more than a rub but less than a marinade. They should be rubbed onto meat, and allowed to sit for at least 20 minutes, or about the same amount of time it takes for a grill to heat. Pastes are highly concentrated in the same way as rubs, but they also contain some perishable ingredients for accent flavors so they are moist. Many pastes have oil added to create the proper thick texture.

---

3 tablespoons dried tarragon

2 tablespoons dried thyme

2 tablespoons grated lemon zest

4 garlic cloves, peeled and pressed through a garlic press

2 teaspoons freshly ground black pepper

3 tablespoons olive oil

Lemon Herb Paste

Yield: ½ cup | Active time: 10 minutes | Start to finish: 10 minutes | Uses: Chicken, fish and seafood, pork, veal

Combine tarragon, thyme, lemon zest, garlic, and pepper in a bowl, and mix well. Add oil, and mix into a paste. Store in an air-tight container, refrigerated, for up to 3 days.

---

1 (2-ounce) tube anchovy paste

6 garlic cloves, peeled and pushed through a garlic press

1 tablespoon Dijon mustard

2 teaspoons herbes de Provence

½ teaspoon freshly ground black pepper

¼ cup extra-virgin olive oil

Provençal Paste

Yield: ½ cup | Active time: 10 minutes | Start to finish: 10 minutes | Uses: Fish and seafood, chicken

Combine anchovy paste, garlic, mustard, herbes de Provence, and pepper in a bowl, and mix well. Add oil, and mix into a paste. Store in an air-tight container, refrigerated, for up to 3 days.

---

3 tablespoons grated fresh ginger

5 garlic cloves, peeled and pressed through a garlic press

2 tablespoons ground cumin

2 tablespoons turmeric

1 tablespoon ground cardamom

½ teaspoon cayenne

4 tablespoons olive oil

Tandoori Paste

Yield: ½ cup | Active time: 10 minutes | Start to finish: 10 minutes | Uses: Beef, lamb, chicken, fish and seafood

Combine ginger, garlic, cumin, turmeric, cardamom, and cayenne in a bowl, and mix well. Add oil, and mix into a paste. Store in an air-tight container, refrigerated, for up to 3 days.

Marinades

Marinades are a time-honored stalwart of cooking. If given enough time, food will definitely absorb the flavor, and marinades can also render less expensive cuts of meat buttery tender. To tenderize, some sort of acid must be present. Vinegars, with the exception of rice wine and balsamic, are too strong; wines and citrus juices are far more delicate, and the food will have a complex flavor from the combination of ingredients rather than having any one dominate.

The following chart will give you some general guidelines to marinating different types of food. Keep in mind that the thinner the food, the less time needed to achieve a meaningful flavor. Also, heartier foods require longer than delicate foods.

Marinating Foods: How Much and For How Long		
FOOD	LIQUID PER POUND	TIME
Beef	½ cup	3–24 hours
Lamb	½ cup	3–24 hours
Pork	½ cup	2–12 hours
Veal	½ cup	1–3 hours
Chicken, with skin and bones	⅓ cup	4–12 hours
Chicken breasts, boneless and skinless	⅓ cup	30 minutes–3 hours
Turkey, whole	1 cup	24 hours
Turkey breast cutlets	⅓ cup	30 minutes–3 hours
Duck, whole	½ cup	4–24 hours
Delicately flavored fish fillets (sole, halibut), and shellfish	¼ cup	30 minutes
Strongly flavored fish fillets/steaks (tuna, bluefish)	¼–½ cup	30 minutes–1 hour
Tender vegetables (mushrooms)	¼ cup	1–2 hours
Thick-skinned vegetables (peppers, eggplant)	¼ cup	2–4 hours

11

6 scallions, white parts and 3 inches of green tops, rinsed, trimmed, and sliced

3 jalapeño or serrano chiles, seeds and ribs removed, and diced

3 garlic cloves, peeled

½ cup vegetable oil

¼ cup soy sauce

2 tablespoons freshly squeezed lime juice

1 teaspoon ground allspice

2 teaspoons granulated sugar

1½ teaspoons dried thyme

½ teaspoon ground cinnamon

½ teaspoon ground ginger

Freshly ground black pepper to taste

Jamaican Jerk Marinade

Yield: 1 cup | Active time: 15 minutes | Start to finish: 15 minutes | Uses: Pork, chicken

Combine scallions, chiles, garlic, vegetable oil, soy sauce, lime juice, allspice, sugar, thyme, cinnamon, ginger, and pepper in a food processor fitted with a steel blade or in a blender. Puree until smooth. Transfer mixture to a heavy resealable plastic bag, add food to be marinated, turning the bag to coat food evenly. Marinate food according to chart above.

Note: The marinade can be refrigerated for up to 3 days, tightly covered.

¼ cup freshly squeezed lime juice

3 tablespoons tequila

2 tablespoons triple sec

1 large jalapeño or serrano chile, seeds and ribs removed, and finely chopped

2 garlic cloves, peeled and minced

2 teaspoons grated lime zest

1 tablespoon chili powder

1 teaspoon ground cumin

1 teaspoon granulated sugar

Salt and freshly ground black pepper to taste

¼ cup vegetable oil

Margarita Mexican Marinade

Yield: ¾ cup | Active time: 10 minutes | Start to finish: 10 minutes | Uses: Chicken, fish and seafood

Combine lime juice, tequila, triple sec, chile, garlic, lime zest, chili powder, cumin, sugar, salt, and pepper in a heavy resealable plastic bag, and mix well. Add oil, and mix well again. Add food to be marinated, turning the bag to coat food evenly. Marinate food according to chart above.

Note: The marinade can be refrigerated for up to 3 days, tightly covered.

Hearty Red Wine Marinade

Yield: 1 cup | Active time: 10 minutes | Start to finish: 10 minutes | Uses: Beef, lamb, venison

Combine wine, vinegar, gin, brown sugar, thyme, rosemary, garlic, orange zest, lemon zest, bay leaves, cloves, salt, and pepper in a heavy resealable plastic bag, and mix well. Add oil, and mix well again. Add food to be marinated, turning the bag to coat food evenly. Marinate food according to chart above.

Note: The marinade can be refrigerated for up to 3 days, tightly covered.

- ½ cup dry red wine
- 2 tablespoons balsamic vinegar
- 2 tablespoons gin
- 2 tablespoons firmly packed dark brown sugar
- 2 tablespoons chopped fresh thyme or 2 teaspoons dried
- 2 tablespoons chopped fresh rosemary or 2 teaspoons dried
- 3 garlic cloves, peeled and minced
- 2 teaspoons grated orange zest
- 1 teaspoon grated lemon zest
- 2 bay leaves, crumbled
- ¼ teaspoon ground cloves
- Salt and freshly ground black pepper to taste
- ¼ cup olive oil

Beer Marinade

Yield: 1 cup | Active time: 5 minutes | Start to finish: 5 minutes | Uses: Chicken, fish and seafood

Combine beer, lemon juice, Worcestershire sauce, garlic, thyme, salt, and pepper sauce in a heavy resealable plastic bag, and mix well. Add oil, and mix well again. Add food to be marinated, turning the bag to coat food evenly. Marinate food according to chart above.

Note: The marinade can be refrigerated for up to 3 days, tightly covered.

- ¾ cup lager beer
- 3 tablespoons freshly squeezed lemon juice
- 1 tablespoon Worcestershire sauce
- 3 garlic cloves, peeled and minced
- 1 tablespoon fresh thyme or 1 teaspoon dried
- Salt and hot red pepper sauce to taste
- 3 tablespoons olive oil

¼ cup mirin or plum wine *

2 tablespoons soy sauce

2 tablespoons orange juice concentrate, thawed

4 garlic cloves, peeled and minced

1 tablespoon Chinese chile paste with garlic *

2 teaspoons grated orange zest

2 tablespoons vegetable oil

2 tablespoons Asian sesame oil*

*Available in the Asian aisle of most supermarkets and in specialty markets.

¼ cup freshly squeezed lemon juice

3 tablespoons chopped fresh rosemary or 1 tablespoon dried

3 tablespoons chopped fresh parsley

2 teaspoons grated lemon zest

3 garlic cloves, peeled and minced

Salt and freshly ground black pepper to taste

⅓ cup olive oil

Spicy Asian Orange Marinade

Yield: ¾ cup | Active time: 5 minutes | Start to finish: 5 minutes | Uses: Pork, chicken, fish and seafood

Combine mirin, soy sauce, orange juice concentrate, garlic, chile paste, and orange zest in a heavy resealable plastic bag, and mix well. Add vegetable oil and sesame oil, and mix well again. Add food to be marinated, turning the bag to coat food evenly. Marinate food according to chart above.

Note: The marinade can be refrigerated for up to 3 days, tightly covered.

Lemon and Rosemary Marinade

Yield: ¾ cup | Active time: 10 minutes | Start to finish: 10 minutes | Uses: Lamb, veal, pork, chicken, fish and seafood

Combine lemon juice, rosemary, parsley, lemon zest, garlic, salt, and pepper in a heavy resealable plastic bag, and mix well. Add oil, and mix well again. Add food to be marinated, turning the bag to coat food evenly. Marinate food according to chart above.

Note: The marinade can be refrigerated for up to 3 days, tightly covered.

Spices are used around the world and add vibrant color as well as flavor to foods.

Brines

Brining, along with smoking and salting, is the way that food was preserved prior to refrigeration and freezing. As is true with marinating, the larger the piece of food, the longer it will take to absorb the flavors. Pork chops need to be soaked for only 8–12 hours, while a whole turkey should be brined for the better part of 2 days.

Apple Cider Brine

Yield: 2 quarts | Active time: 10 minutes | Start to finish: 15 minutes | Uses: Pork, chicken, turkey

1. Combine salt, sugar, apple juice concentrate, cloves, nutmeg, cinnamon sticks, and 1 cup water in a large non-reactive saucepan, and stir well. Bring to a boil over medium-high heat, stirring occasionally. Reduce the heat to low and simmer 2 minutes.

2. Add remaining water to the pan, and allow brine to cool. Transfer brine to a large container, and add food to be brined. Cover and refrigerate.

1 cup kosher salt

½ cup granulated sugar

1 (6-ounce) can apple juice concentrate, thawed

2 tablespoons whole cloves

3 whole nutmeg, crushed

4 cinnamon sticks, crushed

7 cups cold water

Brown Sugar Brine

Yield: 2 quarts | Active time: 5 minutes | Start to finish: 10 minutes | Uses: Pork, chicken, turkey

1. Combine salt, brown sugar, thyme, sage, peppercorns, and 1 cup water in a large non-reactive saucepan, and stir well. Bring to a boil over medium-high heat, stirring occasionally. Reduce the heat to low and simmer 2 minutes.

2. Add remaining water to the pan, and allow brine to cool. Transfer brine to a large container, and add food to be brined. Cover and refrigerate.

1 cup kosher salt

1 cup firmly packed dark brown sugar

¼ cup fresh thyme or 2 tablespoons dried

¼ cup chopped fresh sage or 2 tablespoons dried

3 tablespoons black peppercorns

2 quarts cold water

Chile Brine

Yield: 2 quarts | Active time: 10 minutes | Start to finish: 15 minutes | Uses: Pork, chicken, turkey

1. Combine salt, honey, vinegar, chiles, red pepper flakes, and 1 cup water in a large non-reactive saucepan, and stir well. Bring to a boil over medium-high heat, stirring occasionally. Reduce the heat to low and simmer 2 minutes.

2. Add remaining water to the pan, and allow brine to cool. Transfer brine to a large container, and add food to be brined. Cover and refrigerate.

1 cup kosher salt

1½ cups honey

½ cup cider vinegar

2 jalapeño or serrano chiles, halved

1 tablespoon crushed red pepper flakes

6 cups cold water

Chapter 3

Sauces for Basting and Topping

There are chapters later in this book devoted to specific dishes, many of which have sauces to top the food after it comes off the grill. The recipes in this chapter are for sauces that can be served successfully on a wide variety of foods that are grilled without one of the flavoring methods detailed in Chapter 2. The foods are simple so the sauces make them special.

1 (20-ounce) bottle ketchup

1 cup cider vinegar

½ cup firmly packed dark brown sugar

5 tablespoons Worcestershire sauce

¼ cup vegetable oil

2 tablespoons dry mustard

2 garlic cloves, peeled and minced

1 tablespoon grated fresh ginger

1 lemon, thinly sliced

½–1 teaspoon hot red pepper sauce, or to taste

My Favorite Barbecue Sauce

Yield: 4 cups | Active time: 10 minutes | Start to finish: 40 minutes | Uses: Meat and poultry

1. Combine ketchup, vinegar, brown sugar, Worcestershire sauce, vegetable oil, mustard, garlic, ginger, lemon, and red pepper sauce in a heavy 2-quart saucepan, and bring to a boil over medium heat, stirring occasionally.

2. Reduce the heat to low and simmer sauce, uncovered, for 30 minutes, or until thick, stirring occasionally. Strain sauce, pressing with the back of a spoon to extract as much liquid as possible. Ladle sauce into containers and refrigerate, tightly covered.

Note: The sauce can be made up to 1 week in advance and refrigerated, tightly covered. Bring it back to room temperature before serving.

My Favorite Barbecue Sauce

Kansas City BBQ Sauce

Yield: 2 cups | Active time: 5 minutes | Start to finish: 5 minutes | Uses: Ribs, pork, chicken

Combine ketchup, vinegar, brown sugar, Worcestershire sauce, oil, garlic, ginger, mustard, allspice, cayenne, salt, and pepper in a mixing bowl, and whisk well. Scrape into a container.

Note: The sauce can be refrigerated for up to 1 week. Allow it to reach room temperature before using.

1 cup ketchup

½ cup cider vinegar

¼ cup firmly packed dark brown sugar

2 tablespoons Worcestershire sauce

2 tablespoons vegetable oil

2 garlic cloves, peeled and pushed through a garlic press

½ teaspoon ground ginger

½ teaspoon dry mustard

¼ teaspoon ground allspice

¼ teaspoon cayenne

Salt and freshly ground black pepper to taste

Instant Asian Barbecue Sauce

Yield: 2 cups | Active time: 10 minutes | Start to finish: 10 minutes | Uses: Poultry, fish and seafood, vegetables

Combine applesauce, hoisin sauce, brown sugar, ketchup, honey, rice vinegar, soy sauce, and chile paste in a mixing bowl. Whisk until smooth. Refrigerate until ready to use.

Note: The sauce can be made up to 3 days in advance and refrigerated, tightly covered.

¾ cup unsweetened applesauce

½ cup hoisin sauce *

¼ cup firmly packed dark brown sugar

6 tablespoons ketchup

2 tablespoons honey

2 tablespoons rice vinegar

1 tablespoon soy sauce

1 tablespoon Chinese chile paste with garlic,* or to taste (or substitute hot red pepper sauce)

* Available in the Asian aisle of most supermarkets and in specialty markets.

Balsamic Vinaigrette

Yield: 1½ cups | Active time: 5 minutes | Start to finish: 5 minutes | Uses: Poultry, fish and seafood, vegetables

Combine shallots, garlic, vinegar, mustard, parsley, herbes de Provence, salt, and pepper in a jar with a tight-fitting lid, and shake well. Add olive oil, and shake well again.

Note: The dressing can be made up to 3 days in advance and refrigerated, tightly covered. Bring it back to room temperature before using.

2 shallots, peeled and finely chopped

3 garlic cloves, peeled and minced

⅓ cup balsamic vinegar

2 tablespoons Dijon mustard

1 tablespoon chopped fresh parsley

2 teaspoons herbes de Provence

Salt and freshly ground black pepper to taste

¾ cup extra-virgin olive oil

¼ cup olive oil

1 medium onion, peeled and finely chopped

4 garlic cloves, peeled and minced

1 carrot, peeled and finely chopped

1 celery rib, rinsed, trimmed, and finely chopped

1 (28-ounce) can crushed tomatoes

2 tablespoons chopped fresh parsley

2 tablespoons chopped fresh oregano or 2 teaspoons dried

1 tablespoon fresh thyme or 1 teaspoon dried

2 bay leaves

Salt and crushed red pepper flakes to taste

Herbed Tomato Sauce

Yield: 2 cups | Active time: 15 minutes | Start to finish: 1 hour | Uses: Meats, poultry, fish and seafood, vegetables

1. Heat olive oil in a 2-quart saucepan over medium heat. Add onion and garlic and cook, stirring frequently, for 3 minutes, or until onion is translucent.

2. Add carrot, celery, tomatoes, parsley, oregano, thyme, and bay leaves. Bring to a boil, reduce heat to low, and simmer sauce, uncovered, stirring occasionally, for 40 minutes, or until lightly thickened. Season to taste with salt and red pepper flakes.

Note: The sauce can be made up to 3 days in advance and refrigerated, tightly covered. Bring back to a simmer before serving. It can also be frozen for up to 3 months.

Herbed Tomato Sauce

1½ cups crème fraîche

½ cup prepared white horseradish

¼ cup chopped fresh chives

2 tablespoons freshly squeezed lemon juice

1 teaspoon fresh thyme or ¼ teaspoon dried thyme

Salt and freshly ground black pepper to taste

Horseradish Sauce

Yield: 2 cups | Active time: 10 minutes | Start to finish: 10 minutes | Uses: Beef, lamb

Combine crème fraîche, horseradish, chives, lemon juice, and thyme in a mixing bowl. Stir well, and season to taste with salt and pepper. Refrigerate until ready to use.

Note: The sauce can be made up to 3 days in advance and refrigerated, tightly covered. Bring it back to room temperature before serving.

Blue Cheese Sauce

Yield: 1½ cups | Active time: 5 minutes | Start to finish: 5 minutes | Uses: Meats, poultry, fish and seafood, vegetables

Combine mayonnaise, sour cream, and vinegar in a mixing bowl, and whisk until smooth. Stir in the blue cheese, and season to taste with salt and pepper. Refrigerate until well chilled.

Note: The sauce can be made up to 3 days in advance and refrigerated, tightly covered.

¾ cup mayonnaise

½ cup sour cream

2 tablespoons white wine vinegar

⅓ pound blue cheese, crumbled

Salt and freshly ground black pepper to taste

Greek Feta Sauce

Yield: 1½ cups | Active time: 10 minutes | Start to finish: 10 minutes | Uses: Fish and seafood, poultry, vegetables

Combine feta, sour cream, yogurt, olive oil, lemon juice, and garlic in a food processor fitted with a steel blade or in a blender. Puree until smooth. Scrape mixture into a mixing bowl, and stir in dill. Season to taste with salt and pepper, and refrigerate sauce until ready to use.

Note: The sauce can be made up to 3 days in advance and refrigerated, tightly covered. Bring it back to room temperature before serving.

½ pound mild feta cheese, diced

½ cup sour cream

¼ cup plain whole milk yogurt, preferably Greek

¼ cup extra-virgin olive oil

2 tablespoons freshly squeezed lemon juice

2 garlic cloves, peeled

¼ cup chopped fresh dill or 2 tablespoons dried

Salt and freshly ground black pepper to taste

Spicy Thai Peanut Sauce

Yield: 2 cups | Active time: 10 minutes | Start to finish: 30 minutes, including 20 minutes for chilling | Uses: Meats, poultry, fish and seafood, vegetables

Combine peanut butter, water, brown sugar, lime juice, soy sauce, sesame oil, and chile paste in a mixing bowl. Whisk until well combined. Stir in garlic, scallions, and cilantro, and chill well before serving.

Note: The sauce can be made up to 3 days in advance and refrigerated, tightly covered. Bring it back to room temperature before serving.

1 cup chunky peanut butter

½ cup very hot tap water

½ cup firmly packed dark brown sugar

⅓ cup freshly squeezed lime juice

¼ cup soy sauce

2 tablespoons Asian sesame oil*

2 tablespoons Chinese chile paste with garlic *

6 garlic cloves, peeled and minced

3 scallions, rinsed, trimmed, and chopped

¼ cup chopped fresh cilantro

* Available in the Asian aisle of most supermarkets and in specialty markets.

½ medium cucumber, peeled, seeded, and finely chopped

2 ripe plum tomatoes, rinsed, cored, seeded, and finely chopped

2 scallions, white parts and 3 inches of green tops, rinsed, trimmed, and finely chopped

2 garlic cloves, peeled and minced

1 cup plain whole-milk yogurt

2 tablespoons chopped fresh dill or 2 teaspoons dried

2 tablespoons freshly squeezed lemon juice

Salt and freshly ground black pepper to taste

Dilled Cucumber Raita

Yield: 2 cups | Active time: 10 minutes | Start to finish: 10 minutes | Uses: Meats, poultry, fish and seafood

Combine cucumber, tomatoes, scallions, garlic, yogurt, dill, and lemon juice in a mixing bowl. Stir well, and season to taste with salt and pepper. Refrigerate until ready to use.

Note: The sauce can be made up to 3 days in advance and refrigerated, tightly covered.

2 tablespoons olive oil

½ small red onion, peeled and finely chopped

2 garlic cloves, peeled and minced

2 tablespoons ground cumin

3 (4-ounce) cans chopped mild green chiles, drained

1 cup chicken stock or vegetable stock

1 tablespoon cold water

2 teaspoons cornstarch

3 tablespoons chopped fresh cilantro

Salt and freshly ground black pepper to taste

Quick Green Chile Sauce

Yield: 2 cups | Active time: 10 minutes | Start to finish: 25 minutes | Uses: Meats, poultry, fish and seafood, vegetables

1. Heat olive oil in a 2-quart heavy saucepan over medium-high heat. Add onion and garlic and cook, stirring frequently, for 3 minutes, or until onion is translucent. Reduce the heat to low, stir in cumin, and cook, stirring constantly, for 1 minute.

2. Stir in chiles and stock. Whisk well, bring to a boil, and simmer, uncovered, for 15 minutes, stirring occasionally, or until reduced by one-quarter. Combine cold water and cornstarch in a small bowl, and stir to dissolve cornstarch. Add to sauce, and bring to a simmer, stirring constantly. Cook over low heat for 1–2 minutes, or until sauce thickens.

3. Stir in cilantro, and season to taste with salt and pepper. Serve hot or at room temperature.

Note: The sauce can be made up to 3 days in advance and refrigerated, tightly covered. Bring it back to room temperature or to a simmer before serving.

Chapter 4
Hors d'Oeuvres and Appetizers

When you have the grill lit for the main course of a meal, it only makes sense to utilize this versatile cooking tool for more than one dish. In this chapter you will find recipes for small nibbles to enjoy with a cocktail or glass of wine before dinner, as well as small first courses—most of them seafood—to serve at the table. Many of the recipes in this chapter are excellent for buffet entertaining and cocktail parties too. In addition to the dishes in this chapter, also take a look at the soups and salads in Chapter 5 for other light options to begin a meal.

Chicken Satay with Spicy Thai Peanut Sauce

Yield: 36 pieces | Active time: 15 minutes | Start to finish: 3¼ hours, including 3 hours for marinating

1. Trim fat from chicken breasts and pull off tenderloins. Remove tendon from the center of each tenderloin by holding down tip with your finger and scraping away meat with the dull side of a paring knife. Cut tenderloins in half, and cut the remaining chicken meat into 1-inch cubes.

2. Combine soy sauce, brown sugar, lime juice, chile paste, garlic, and sesame oil in a heavy resealable plastic bag, and blend well. Add chicken pieces and marinate, refrigerated, for 3 hours, turning the bag occasionally.

3. Prepare a medium-hot grill according to the instructions given in Chapter 1.

4. Remove chicken from marinade, and discard marinade. Grill chicken pieces, uncovered if using a charcoal grill, turning pieces with tongs, for a total of 3–5 minutes or until brown and cooked through. Spear each piece of chicken with a toothpick or bamboo skewer and serve hot with a cup of Spicy Thai Peanut Sauce for dipping.

VARIATION: *Cubes of pork or beef, large shrimp, or strips of salmon can become satay as well as chicken.*

Note: The chicken can marinate for up to 6 hours, and it can be cooked 1 day in advance and refrigerated, tightly covered. Reheat it in a 350°F oven wrapped in aluminum foil for 5–10 minutes, or until hot.

4 boneless and skinless chicken breast halves

½ cup soy sauce

½ cup firmly packed dark brown sugar

¼ cup freshly squeezed lime juice

2 tablespoons Chinese chile paste with garlic *

4 garlic cloves, peeled and minced

1 tablespoon Asian sesame oil*

1 cup Spicy Thai Peanut Sauce (recipe on page 19)

* Available in the Asian aisle of most supermarkets and in specialty markets.

1 navel orange

3 scallions, trimmed and cut into 2-inch sections

6 garlic cloves, peeled

4 (¼-inch-thick) slices peeled fresh ginger

¼ cup soy sauce

¼ cup Asian sesame oil *

Freshly ground black pepper to taste

24 chicken wing drumettes

* Available in the Asian aisle of most supermarkets and in specialty markets.

Chinese Chicken Wings

Yield: 24 pieces | Active time: 15 minutes | Start to finish: 6½ hours, including 6 hours for marinating

1. Remove zest from orange with a sharp paring knife. Squeeze juice from orange, and set aside.

2. Place zest, scallions, garlic, and ginger in a food processor fitted with a steel blade or in a blender. Puree until smooth. Scrape mixture into a heavy resealable plastic bag, add orange juice, soy sauce, sesame oil, and pepper, and mix well. Add chicken wings.

3. Marinate chicken wings, refrigerated, for at least 6 hours, preferably overnight, turning the bag occasionally.

4. Prepare a medium-hot grill according to the instructions given in Chapter 1.

5. Remove wings from marinade and discard marinade. Grill wings, covered, for a total of 10–15 minutes, turning them occasionally with tongs, or until cooked through and no longer pink. Serve hot, at room temperature, or chilled.

Note: The wings can be grilled 1 day in advance and refrigerated, tightly covered.

Chinese Chicken Wings

22

Tomato and Olive Bruschetta

Yield: 24 pieces | Active time: 20 minutes | Start to finish: 50 minutes

1. Prepare a medium-hot grill according to the instructions given in Chapter 1.

2. Brush onion with olive oil. Grill onion, turning with tongs occasionally, for 12–15 minutes, or until onion is tender.

3. While onion grills, brush bread slices with oil, and grill for 2 minutes per side, or until toasted. Cut 1 garlic clove in half, and rub on 1 side of toast. Set aside.

4. Discarding root end, chop onion. Mince remaining 2 garlic cloves. Combine onion, garlic, tomatoes, feta, olives, chiles, paprika, cumin, and remaining olive oil in a mixing bowl. Season to taste with salt and pepper.

5. To serve, mound topping on toast slices, and serve immediately.

Note: The topping and the toast slices can be prepared up to 3 hours in advance and kept at room temperature.

1 small red onion, peeled and halved lengthwise

¼ cup olive oil, divided

24 slices French or Italian bread, ½ inch thick

3 garlic cloves, peeled

5 ripe plum tomatoes, cored, seeded, and finely chopped

¼ cup crumbled feta cheese

¼ cup chopped black olives

2 tablespoons chopped mild green chiles, drained

1 teaspoon smoked Spanish paprika

½ teaspoon ground cumin

Salt and freshly ground black pepper to taste

Tomato and Olive Bruschetta

2 pounds large sea scallops, rinsed and patted dry with paper towels

¼ cup olive oil, divided

Salt and freshly ground black pepper to taste

1 navel orange

¼ cup freshly squeezed lime juice

½ English cucumber, cut into ⅓-inch dice

¼ small red onion, peeled and chopped

1 small jalapeño or serrano chile, seeds and ribs removed, and finely chopped

¼ cup chopped fresh cilantro

3–4 cups mixed salad greens, rinsed and dried

Marinated Sea Scallops

Yield: 6–8 servings | Active time: 30 minutes | Start to finish: 2 hours, including 45 minutes for marinating

1. Prepare a hot grill according to the instructions given in Chapter 1.

2. Toss scallops with 2 tablespoons oil, and season to taste with salt and pepper. Cut peel (including all white pith) from orange using a small serrated knife. Dice orange, and set aside.

3. Grill scallops, uncovered if using a charcoal grill, turning once, until just cooked through, about 5 minutes. Remove scallops from the grill, and allow them to cool. Cut scallops into quarters.

4. Combine scallops, orange, lime juice, cucumber, onion, chile, and remaining oil in a mixing bowl. Season to taste with salt and pepper, and refrigerate scallops, covered, for at least 45 minutes, or until cold.

5. Stir cilantro into scallop mixture. To serve, divide salad greens onto individual plates, and mound scallop mixture in the center.

VARIATION: *Large shrimp or 1-inch cubes of any firm-fleshed white fish such as cod or halibut can be used in place of scallops.*

Note: The scallops can be cooked and the rest of the mixture can be prepared up to 1 day in advance and refrigerated separately, tightly covered. Do not mix scallops into vegetable mixture more than 2 hours in advance.

2 dozen live oysters

4 tablespoons unsalted butter, softened

2 garlic cloves, peeled and minced

3 tablespoons chopped fresh parsley

2 tablespoons chopped fresh chives

Salt and freshly ground black pepper to taste

Grilled Oysters

Yield: 4–6 servings | Active time: 15 minutes | Start to finish: 40 minutes

1. Prepare a medium-hot grill according to the instructions given in Chapter 1. Scrub oysters well under cold running water. Discard any that do not shut tightly while being scrubbed.

2. Combine butter, garlic, parsley, chives, salt, and pepper in a small bowl, and beat until smooth.

3. Place oysters on the grill with rounded side down. Grill, covered, 3–4 minutes. Remove oysters with tongs, and place on a hot pad. Remove and discard top shell with an oyster knife, being careful not to spill oyster liquor. Separate oysters from bottom shell, but do not remove oyster.

24

4. Top each oyster with 2 teaspoons seasoned butter. Return oysters to grill, and cook, covered, for 2–3 minutes more, or until edges of oysters curl. Serve immediately.

VARIATION: *Large littleneck clams can be substituted for the oysters.*

Note: The butter mixture can be prepared up to 3 days in advance and refrigerated, tightly covered with plastic wrap. Allow butter to reach room temperature before using.

Clams Casino

Yield: 4–6 servings | Active time: 20 minutes | Start to finish: 35 minutes

5 tablespoons unsalted butter

¾ cup finely chopped onion

4 garlic cloves, peeled and minced

1 red bell pepper, seeds and ribs removed, finely chopped

1½ cups Italian breadcrumbs

¼ cup freshly grated Parmesan cheese

24 littleneck clams

1. Prepare a medium-hot grill according to the instructions given in Chapter 1.

2. Melt butter in a large skillet over medium heat. Add onion and garlic, and cook, stirring frequently, for 3 minutes, or until onion is translucent. Add red bell pepper and cook, stirring frequently, for 5–7 minutes, or until pepper is soft. Add breadcrumbs and cheese to mixture, and stir to combine. Set aside.

3. Scrub clams well under cold running water. Discard any that do not shut tightly while being scrubbed. Place clams in a mixing bowl, and cover them with very hot tap water. Within about 2 minutes the shells will be slightly apart. Insert a clam knife or paring knife between the shells at one corner, and sever the muscles holding the shells together.

4. Mound topping on clams, using about 1 tablespoon per clam. Grill for 5–8 minutes, covered, depending on the size of the clam, or until the clams are hot. Serve immediately.

Note: The topping can be made up to 2 days in advance and refrigerated in a container or heavy plastic bag.

1 cup mesquite chips

4 ears fresh corn, unshucked

¾ pound bulk pork sausage

½ cup finely chopped red bell pepper

½ cup finely chopped green bell pepper

3 scallions, white parts and 2 inches of green tops, rinsed, trimmed, and finely chopped

3 tablespoons olive oil

2 tablespoons freshly squeezed lime juice

2 tablespoons pure maple syrup

Salt and freshly ground black pepper to taste

3 tablespoons finely chopped fresh cilantro

6–8 leaves romaine, rinsed and dried

Grilled Corn and Sausage Salad

Yield: 6–8 servings | Active time: 15 minutes | Start to finish: 1 hour

1. Prepare a medium-hot grill according to the instructions given in Chapter 1. If using a charcoal grill, soak mesquite chips in water for 30 minutes. If using a gas grill, create a packet for wood chips as described in Chapter 1.

2. Remove all but 1 layer of husks from corn and pull out the corn silks. Soak corn in cold water to cover for 10 minutes. Place wood chips on the grill. Grill corn, covered, for 10–15 minutes, turning with tongs occasionally.

3. When cool enough to handle, discard husks, and cut kernels off cobs using a sharp serrated knife.

4. Cook sausage in a frying pan over medium heat, breaking up lumps with a fork. Cook until brown. Combine sausage and its fat with corn, red and green bell peppers, and scallions in a mixing bowl.

5. Combine olive oil, lime juice, maple syrup, salt, and pepper in a jar with a tight-fitting lid. Shake well, and toss with the corn mixture. Toss with cilantro, and serve at room temperature on top of lettuce leaves.

Note: The salad can be made up to 2 days in advance and refrigerated, tightly covered with plastic wrap. Allow it to sit at room temperature for a few hours to take the chill off. Do not add the cilantro until just before serving.

Chapter 5

Soups and Small Vegetable Salads

Hot soups to warm you in winter or chilly soups to cool you in summer are always a welcome way to begin a meal, or a satisfying focus of a light supper or lunch. Most of the recipes in this chapter include component parts that spend some time cooking on the grill, so their aroma and flavor permeates the broth.

Small vegetable salads are another starter as versatile as they are delicious (for grilled salad entrees, see Chapter 11). All of the salad recipes in this chapter can become part of a buffet dinner.

Grilled Corn Soup

Yield: 6–8 servings | Active time: 20 minutes | Start to finish: 1 hour

1 cup mesquite chips
4 large garlic cloves, unpeeled
8–10 medium ears fresh corn, unshucked
2 tablespoons unsalted butter
¼ cup yellow cornmeal
2 cups chicken stock
2 cups whole milk
Salt and freshly ground black pepper to taste

1. Prepare a medium-hot grill according to the instructions given in Chapter 1. If using a charcoal grill, soak mesquite chips in water for 30 minutes. If using a gas grill, create a packet for wood chips as described in Chapter 1.

2. Preheat the oven to 350°F. Bake garlic cloves for 15 minutes, and peel garlic when cool enough to handle. Set aside.

3. Remove all but 1 layer of husks from the corn, and pull out corn silks. Soak corn in cold water to cover for 10 minutes. Place mesquite chips on the grill. Grill corn, covered, for 10–15 minutes, turning with tongs occasionally. Remove corn from the grill, and when cool enough to handle, cut kernels from cobs with a sharp serrated knife.

4. Melt butter in a large saucepan, and cook kernels over low heat for 5 minutes, stirring occasionally. Remove 1 cup of kernels, and set aside. Puree remaining corn, roasted garlic, cornmeal, and stock in a food processor fitted with a steel blade or in a blender. This will probably have to be done in a few batches.

5. Combine puree with milk and heat to a boil over medium heat. Add reserved corn kernels, and season to taste with salt and pepper. Reduce the heat to low, and simmer for 5 minutes, stirring occasionally.

Note: The soup can be made up to 2 days in advance and refrigerated, tightly covered. Reheat soup slowly, but do not let it boil or reduce. After it has been chilled, it may have to be thinned with a little additional milk or stock.

1 Japanese eggplant, trimmed and cut lengthwise into ½-inch slices

1 zucchini, trimmed and cut lengthwise into ½-inch slices

1 yellow squash, trimmed and cut lengthwise into ½-inch slices

1 medium sweet onion, such as Vidalia or Bermuda, peeled and cut into ½-inch slices

1 large red bell pepper, seeds and ribs removed, and cut lengthwise into quarters

¼ cup olive oil

Salt and freshly ground black pepper to taste

2 garlic cloves, peeled and minced

4 cups chicken stock

1 (14.5-ounce) can diced tomatoes, drained

¼ cup chopped fresh parsley

2 tablespoons chopped fresh oregano or 2 teaspoons dried

Farmer's Market Vegetable Soup

Yield: 4–6 servings | Active time: 20 minutes | Start to finish: 1 hour

1. Prepare a medium-hot grill according to the instructions given in Chapter 1.

2. Brush eggplant, zucchini, yellow squash, onion, and bell pepper slices with olive oil, reserving 1 tablespoon. Sprinkle vegetables with salt and pepper.

3. Grill vegetables, covered, for a total of 8 minutes, turning them once. Remove vegetables from the grill. Peel pepper, and then cut all vegetables into a ½-inch dice.

4. Heat remaining oil in a heavy 2-quart saucepan over medium-high heat. Add garlic, and cook, stirring constantly, for 1 minute. Add stock, tomatoes, parsley, oregano, and diced vegetables, and bring to a boil. Reduce the heat to low, and simmer soup, uncovered, for 15 minutes, stirring occasionally. Serve immediately.

Note: The soup can be made up to 2 days in advance and refrigerated, tightly covered. Reheat soup slowly, but do not let it boil or reduce.

Farmer's Market Vegetable Soup

Smoked Garlic Soup

Yield: 4–6 servings | Active time: 20 minutes | Start to finish: 1½ hours

1 cup apple wood or mesquite chips

4 large heads garlic

2 tablespoons olive oil

2 tablespoons unsalted butter

1 large onion, peeled and diced

1 tablespoon fresh thyme or 1 teaspoon dried

5 cups chicken stock

¾ cup heavy cream

Salt and freshly ground black pepper to taste

½ cup freshly grated Parmesan cheese

1. Prepare a medium grill according to the instructions given in Chapter 1. If using a charcoal grill, soak apple wood or mesquite chips in water for 30 minutes. If using a gas grill, create a packet for wood chips as described in Chapter 1.

2. Cut top ½ inch off of garlic heads, and rub oil all over heads, including cut surfaces. Cut 4 (6-inch) squares of heavy-duty aluminum foil, and wrap them around garlic, allowing the top cut surface to show.

3. Place wood chips on the grill. Grill garlic, covered, for 25 minutes, or until cloves are soft when pressed with the tip of a paring knife. Remove garlic from the grill, and when cool enough to handle, pop cloves out of husks and set aside.

4. Melt butter in 2-quart heavy saucepan over medium-high heat. Add onion and thyme, and cook, stirring frequently, for 3 minutes, or until onion is translucent. Add garlic, stock, and cream, and bring to a boil over medium-high heat.

5. Reduce the heat to low and simmer soup, uncovered, for 15 minutes, stirring occasionally. Puree soup in a food processor fitted with a steel blade or in a blender; this may have to be done in batches. Season soup to taste with salt and pepper.

6. To serve, divide grated cheese among soup bowls and ladle soup over cheese. Serve immediately.

Note: The soup can be made up to 2 days in advance and refrigerated, tightly covered. Reheat soup slowly, but do not let it boil or reduce.

3 tablespoons unsalted
  butter

2 leeks, white and pale
  green parts, rinsed,
  trimmed, and thinly sliced

2 carrots, peeled and thinly
  sliced

2 celery ribs, rinsed,
  trimmed, and thinly sliced

2 cups chicken stock

1 tablespoon fresh thyme
  or 1 teaspoon dried

1 bay leaf

2 cups whole milk

1 (12-ounce) bottle
  or can beer

1 tablespoon
  Worcestershire sauce

1 teaspoon dry mustard

2 tablespoons cornstarch

3 tablespoons cold water

4 cups (1 pound) grated
  extra-sharp cheddar
  cheese

Salt and freshly ground
  black pepper to taste

Wisconsin Cheddar Beer Soup

Yield: 6–8 servings | Active time: 20 minutes | Start to finish: 1 hour

1. Heat butter in a heavy saucepan over medium-high heat. Add leeks, carrots, and celery, and cook, stirring frequently, for 3 minutes, or until leeks are translucent. Add stock, thyme, and bay leaf, and bring to a boil. Reduce the heat to low, and simmer soup, uncovered, for 30 minutes, or until vegetables are tender. Remove and discard bay leaf.

2. Strain soup, reserving all broth. Place vegetables in a food processor fitted with a steel blade or in a blender, and puree until smooth; add some of reserved stock as necessary.

3. Return stock and vegetable puree to the saucepan, and add milk, beer, Worcestershire sauce, and mustard. Bring to a boil over medium-high heat, then reduce the heat to low and simmer soup, uncovered, for 10 minutes.

4. Combine cornstarch and water in a small bowl, and stir well. Add mixture to soup, and simmer for 2 minutes or until thickened and bubbly. Add cheese to soup in ½-cup measures, stirring well to melt cheese between each addition. Season to taste with salt and pepper, and serve immediately.

Note: The soup can be made up to 2 days in advance and refrigerated, tightly covered. Reheat over low heat, stirring frequently.

Wild Rice, Corn, and Sausage Soup

Yield: 6–8 servings | Active time: 20 minutes | Start to finish: 1 hour

1. Place 2½ cups stock in a saucepan, and bring to a boil over medium-high heat. Add wild rice, reduce the heat to low, and cook rice, covered, for 35–40 minutes, or until puffed and tender.

2. While rice simmers, combine 2 cups corn and 1 cup stock in a food processor fitted with a steel blade or in a blender. Puree until smooth. Heat butter in a saucepan over medium-high heat. Add sausage, onion, carrot, and celery, and cook, stirring frequently, for 3 minutes or until onion is translucent. Add remaining stock, and simmer soup, partially covered, for 15 minutes.

3. Add cooked rice with any stock remaining in the pan, corn puree, and remaining corn to soup. Simmer, partially covered, for 15 minutes. Stir in cream, and simmer 5 minutes. Season to taste with salt and pepper, and serve hot, sprinkled with chives.

Note: The soup can be prepared up to 2 days in advance and refrigerated, tightly covered. Reheat it over low heat, stirring frequently.

Ingredients:

- 6 cups chicken stock, divided
- ⅔ cup wild rice, rinsed well
- 3 cups fresh corn kernels (or frozen kernels, thawed), divided
- 2 tablespoons unsalted butter
- ½ pound cooked smoked sausage, such as kielbasa, cut into ¼-inch dice
- 1 large onion, peeled and diced
- 1 carrot, peeled and diced
- 1 celery rib, rinsed, trimmed, and diced
- ¾ cup light cream
- Salt and freshly ground black pepper to taste
- 3 tablespoons chopped fresh chives

Panzanella Salad

Yield: 4–6 servings | Active time: 20 minutes | Start to finish: 1 hour

1. Prepare a medium-hot grill according to the instructions given in Chapter 1.

2. Combine vinegar, orange juice, 2 garlic cloves, orange zest, salt, and pepper in a jar with a tight-fitting lid, and shake well. Add ½ cup olive oil, and shake well again. Set aside.

3. Place tomatoes in a large salad bowl, and sprinkle liberally with salt and pepper.

4. Brush pepper slices, zucchini, and onion with remaining olive oil. Rub bread slices with remaining garlic. Grill peppers and onion, covered, for a total of 4 minutes, and bread slices and zucchini for a total of 3 minutes, turning slices frequently, or until vegetables are tender and bread is toasted. Remove food from the grill.

5. Cut bread and vegetables into 1-inch pieces, and add to bowl with tomatoes. Toss with dressing, and allow to stand for 15 minutes. Serve immediately, sprinkled with parsley.

Note: The dressing can be prepared up to a day in advance and refrigerated; return to room temperature. Bread and vegetables can be grilled up to 4 hours in advance. Do not combine salad ingredients until 15 minutes before serving.

Ingredients:

- ⅓ cup red wine vinegar
- ¼ cup freshly squeezed orange juice
- 3 garlic cloves, peeled and minced, divided
- 2 teaspoons grated orange zest
- Salt and freshly ground black pepper to taste
- ⅔ cup olive oil, divided
- 1 pound ripe tomatoes, cored and cut into ¾-inch dice
- 2 red, orange, or yellow bell peppers, seeds and ribs removed, and cut into 1-inch strips
- 1 pound zucchini, cut on the diagonal into ⅓-inch slices
- 1 medium red onion, peeled and cut into ¼-inch slices
- 1 (12-ounce) loaf of hearty Italian bread, cut into 1-inch slices
- ¼ cup chopped fresh Italian parsley

⅓ cup olive oil

2 garlic cloves, peeled and minced

2 Japanese eggplants, trimmed and quartered lengthwise

1 zucchini, trimmed and quartered lengthwise

1 yellow squash, trimmed and quartered lengthwise

1 small sweet onion, such as Vidalia or Bermuda, peeled and quartered

¼ pound large mushrooms, wiped clean with a damp paper towel, and stemmed

6 ripe plum tomatoes, rinsed, halved, and seeded

Salt and freshly ground black pepper to taste

¼ cup balsamic vinegar

½ cup chopped fresh oregano

Mixed Vegetable Salad with Oregano

Yield: 4–6 servings | Active time: 20 minutes | Start to finish: 45 minutes

1. Prepare a medium-hot grill according to the instructions given in Chapter 1.

2. Mix olive oil and garlic. Brush oil on both sides of eggplants, zucchini, yellow squash, onion, mushrooms, and tomatoes.

3. Grill all vegetables except tomatoes, covered, for a total of 10 minutes, turning occasionally, or until crisp tender; add tomatoes for last 4 minutes of cooking time. Remove vegetables from the grill with tongs, and, when cool enough to handle, cut vegetables into 1-inch slices.

4. To serve, divide vegetables on individual plates or arrange on a platter. Season to taste with salt and pepper, then drizzle with vinegar and sprinkle with oregano.

Note: The vegetables can be grilled up to 4 hours in advance and kept at room temperature.

Mixed Vegetable Salad with Oregano

Provençal Vegetable Salad with Feta

Yield: 4–6 servings | Active time: 20 minutes | Start to finish: 1 hour

1. Combine salt and water in a large mixing bowl, and submerge eggplant slices; use a plate to press them down into the salted water. Soak eggplant for 30 minutes, then drain slices and squeeze to extract as much water as possible.

2. While eggplant soaks, prepare a medium-hot grill according to the instructions given in Chapter 1.

3. Place eggplant, zucchini, red bell pepper, onion, and mushrooms on baking sheet, keeping vegetables segregated. Drizzle with oil and sprinkle with garlic, herbes de Provence, salt, and pepper. Turn vegetables to coat evenly.

4. Begin by placing onion and red bell pepper on the grill, and 4 minutes later add eggplant, zucchini, and mushrooms. Grill vegetables, covered, until tender and lightly brown, turning slices frequently. Vegetables should cook for a total of 10 minutes.

5. To serve, divide vegetables on individual plates or arrange on a platter. Sprinkle with vinegar, feta, olives, and basil. Serve hot or at room temperature.

Note: The vegetables can be grilled up to 4 hours in advance and kept at room temperature.

- ½ cup kosher salt
- 2 quarts cold water
- 2 (1-pound) eggplants, cut into ¾-inch-thick rounds
- 2 medium zucchini, quartered lengthwise
- 2 red bell peppers, seeds and ribs removed, and cut into 2-inch strips
- 1 large sweet onion, such as Vidalia or Bermuda, peeled and cut into ½-inch slices
- ½ pound large mushrooms, wiped clean with a damp paper towel, trimmed, and halved
- ⅓ cup olive oil
- 4 garlic cloves, peeled and minced
- 3 tablespoons herbes de Provence
- Salt and freshly ground black pepper to taste
- ¼ cup balsamic vinegar
- 1 cup crumbled feta cheese
- ½ cup pitted oil-cured black olives, preferably Provençal
- ¼ cup slivered fresh basil

Chapter 6

Fish and Seafood

While the states of the Midwest are landlocked from both the Atlantic and Pacific oceans, do not count them out when it comes to seafood. The Great Lakes supply myriad aquatic species such as whitefish and walleye pike, and the streams and lakes are plentiful with trout.

While shops only selling fish and seafood are disappearing from the scene, it is worth the effort to search your neighborhood for the best source you can find for fresh fish. Look for a market that offers a varied selection, that keeps its fish on foil placed on top of chipped ice, and that has a level of personal service that allows you to special-order specific varieties or cuts of fish.

4–6 (8-ounce) whitefish fillets with skin

¾ cup olive oil, divided

Salt and freshly ground black pepper to taste

1 cup fish stock or bottled clam juice

¼ cup freshly squeezed lemon juice

¼ cup chopped fresh tarragon

2 tablespoons chopped fresh parsley

Whitefish with Tarragon Sauce

Yield: 4–6 servings | Active time: 20 minutes | Start to finish: 40 minutes

1. Prepare a medium-hot grill according to the instructions given in Chapter 1.

2. Rinse fillets, and pat dry with paper towels. Rub fish with oil, and sprinkle with salt and pepper. Set aside.

3. Boil fish stock or clam juice until it is reduced to ¼ cup. Place stock in a jar with a tight-fitting lid, and add lemon juice, tarragon, parsley, salt, and pepper, and shake well. Add remaining olive oil, and shake well again. Set aside.

4. Cook fish, uncovered if using a charcoal grill, for 5–7 minutes per side, turning gently with a wide spatula, or until fish is opaque at the edges and slightly translucent in the center. Serve immediately, with tarragon sauce on top.

Note: The dressing can be made up to 1 day in advance and refrigerated, tightly covered. Bring it to room temperature before using.

Walleye Pike with Dilled Tomato and Corn Relish

Yield: 4–6 servings | Active time: 20 minutes | Start to finish: 40 minutes

1. Prepare a medium-hot grill according to the instructions given in Chapter 1.

2. Rinse fillets, and pat dry with paper towels. Rub fish with oil, and sprinkle with salt and pepper. Set aside.

3. Combine tomatoes, corn, scallions, and dill in a mixing bowl. Combine vinegar, sugar, salt, and pepper in a small bowl, and stir well. Add remaining oil, and stir well again. Toss dressing with vegetables, and set aside at room temperature.

4. Cook fish, uncovered if using a charcoal grill, for 3–5 minutes per side, turning gently with a wide spatula, or until fish is opaque at the edges and slightly translucent in the center. To serve, place fillets on plates, and top with relish. Serve immediately.

Note: The relish can be made up to 1 day in advance and refrigerated, tightly covered. Bring it to room temperature before using.

4–6 (8-ounce) walleye pike fillets with skin

⅓ cup olive oil, divided

Salt and freshly ground black pepper to taste

2 large ripe tomatoes, rinsed, cored, seeded, and chopped

1 cup fresh corn kernels, cooked, or frozen kernels, thawed

4 scallions, white parts and 2 inches of green tops, rinsed, trimmed, and thinly sliced

3 tablespoons chopped fresh dill

¼ cup white balsamic vinegar or cider vinegar

2 teaspoons granulated sugar

World's Easiest Fish

Yield: 4–6 servings | Active time: 15 minutes | Start to finish: 35 minutes

1. Prepare a medium-hot grill according to the instructions given in Chapter 1.

2. Rinse fish and pat dry with paper towels. Combine mayonnaise, herbs, garlic, salt, and pepper in a mixing bowl, and stir well. Coat both sides of fish steaks with mixture.

3. Grill fish, uncovered if using a charcoal grill, for 3–5 minutes per side, or until cooked through and just slightly translucent in the center. Serve immediately.

4–6 boneless (6–8-ounce) fish steaks or fillets of your choice, at least 1 inch thick

⅔ cup commercial mayonnaise

3 tablespoons chopped fresh herbs (such as oregano, rosemary, tarragon, basil, parsley, or some combination)

2 garlic cloves, peeled and minced

Salt and freshly ground black pepper to taste

4–6 (12-ounce) rainbow trout, scaled and gutted, with heads left on

3 tablespoons olive oil

Salt and freshly ground black pepper to taste

1 lemon

¼ pound (1 stick) unsalted butter

4–6 slices white sandwich bread, crusts trimmed and cut into ½-inch cubes

3 tablespoons chopped fresh parsley

1 tablespoon small capers, drained and rinsed

Rainbow Trout with Lemon Butter Sauce

Yield: 4–6 servings | Active time: 25 minutes | Start to finish: 40 minutes

1. Prepare a medium-hot grill according to the instructions given in Chapter 1.

2. Rinse trout and pat dry with paper towels. Rub fish with oil, and sprinkle with salt and pepper. Cut lemon in half lengthwise, and slice off 4–6 slices from one half. Tuck slices inside of trout. Squeeze juice from remaining portions of lemon, and set aside.

3. Melt butter in a skillet over medium-high heat. Add bread cubes, and cook, turning frequently, until cubes are browned. Remove cubes from the skillet with a slotted spatula, and set aside. Add lemon juice, parsley, and capers to butter, and heat well. Season to taste with salt and pepper, and keep warm.

4. Grill trout for 4 minutes per side, uncovered if using a charcoal grill, or until skin is crisp and flesh is no longer translucent. To serve, top each trout with butter sauce and sprinkle with croutons. Serve immediately.

Note: The butter sauce can be made up to 6 hours in advance and kept at room temperature.

Rainbow Trout with Lemon Butter Sauce

Swordfish with Smoked Cheddar Sauce

Swordfish with Smoked Cheddar Sauce

Yield: 4–6 servings | Active time: 20 minutes | Start to finish: 40 minutes

1. Prepare a dual-temperature hot-and-medium grill according to the instructions given in Chapter 1. Rinse fish and pat dry with paper towels. Sprinkle with salt and pepper, and set aside.

2. Cook bacon in a skillet over medium-high heat until brown. Remove bacon from the pan with a slotted spoon, and discard all but 2 tablespoons bacon fat. Add onion and garlic, and cook over medium heat, stirring frequently, for 3–5 minutes, or until onion is translucent. Add ¾ cup stock and cream. Bring to a boil, and simmer for 5 minutes. Mix cornstarch with reserved stock, stir well, and add to sauce. Stir sauce over low heat until thickened and bubbly. Add cheese, and stir until melted. Add tomato and reserved bacon, and keep sauce warm.

3. Sear fish for 2–3 minutes per side on the hot side of the grill, uncovered if using a charcoal grill, then transfer fish to the cooler side of the grill, and cook for an additional 2–3 minutes per side, or until slightly translucent in the center. Serve immediately, topped with sauce.

Note: The sauce can be prepared up to 2 days in advance and refrigerated, tightly covered. Reheat it in a saucepan over low heat, stirring frequently.

4–6 (6–8-ounce) swordfish steaks

Salt and freshly ground black pepper to taste

½ pound bacon, cut into small pieces

1 medium onion, peeled and chopped

1 garlic clove, peeled and minced

1 cup chicken stock, divided

1 cup heavy cream

2 teaspoons cornstarch

1½ cups grated smoked cheddar cheese

1 medium tomato, peeled, seeded, and finely chopped

4–6 (6–8-ounce) swordfish steaks

½ cup dry white wine

¼ cup freshly squeezed lemon juice

Grated zest from 1 lemon

4 garlic cloves, peeled and minced

1 shallot, peeled and chopped

¼ cup chopped fresh parsley

2 tablespoons dried oregano

1 tablespoon fresh thyme or 1 teaspoon dried

Salt and freshly ground black pepper to taste

½ cup olive oil

Aegean Swordfish

Yield: 4–6 servings | Active time: 15 minutes | Start to finish: 2¼ hours, including 2 hours for marinating

1. Rinse swordfish steaks, and set aside. Combine wine, lemon juice, lemon zest, garlic, shallot, parsley, oregano, thyme, salt, and pepper in a heavy resealable plastic bag and mix well. Add olive oil, and mix well again. Add swordfish and marinate, refrigerated, for 2–3 hours, turning the bag occasionally.

2. Prepare a dual-temperature hot-and-medium grill according to the instructions given in Chapter 1.

3. Remove fish from marinade, and discard marinade. Sear fish for 2–3 minutes per side on the hot side of the grill, uncovered if using a charcoal grill, then transfer fish to the cooler side of the grill, and cook for an additional 2–3 minutes per side, or until slightly translucent in the center. Serve immediately.

VARIATION: *Other firm-fleshed fish, such as sea bass, halibut, or scrod, can be substituted.*

Aegean Swordfish

Salmon Provençal

Yield: 4–6 servings | Active time: 15 minutes | Start to finish: 3½ hours, including 3 hours for marinating

1. Rinse salmon and pat dry with paper towels. Skin salmon by running the blade of a boning knife between the meat and skin.

2. Combine wine, vinegar, mustard, garlic, parsley, herbes de Provence, salt, and pepper in a heavy resalable plastic bag, and mix well. Add olive oil, and mix well again. Add salmon and marinate, refrigerated, for 3–8 hours, turning the bag occasionally.

3. Prepare a medium-hot grill according to the instructions given in Chapter 1. If using a charcoal grill, soak mesquite chips in water for 30 minutes. If using a gas grill, create a packet for wood chips as described in Chapter 1.

4. Remove salmon from marinade, and discard marinade. Place wood chips on the grill. Cook fish, covered, for 3–5 minutes per side, turning gently with a wide spatula, or until fish is opaque at the edges and slightly translucent in the center. Serve immediately.

VARIATION: *Cod, halibut, or sea bass can be substituted for the salmon.*

4–6 (6-ounce) salmon fillets
1 cup dry white wine
¼ cup balsamic vinegar
3 tablespoons Dijon mustard
4 garlic cloves, peeled and minced
2 tablespoons chopped fresh parsley
1 tablespoon herbes de Provence
Salt and freshly ground black pepper to taste
¼ cup olive oil
1 cup mesquite chips

2 pounds jumbo shrimp (less than 10 per pound), unpeeled

2 lemons

4 garlic cloves, peeled

Salt and freshly ground black pepper to taste

⅔ cup extra-virgin olive oil

¼ cup finely chopped fresh oregano

2 tablespoons chopped fresh parsley

Grilled Greek Shrimp

Yield: 4–6 servings | Active time: 20 minutes | Start to finish: 1 hour

1. Prepare a medium-hot grill according to the instructions given in Chapter 1.

2. Using sharp scissors, cut along middle of the back of shrimp; leave tail and first segment intact. Devein shrimp using a sharp paring knife but do not remove shells. Rinse shrimp and pat dry with paper towels.

3. Grate zest and squeeze juice from lemons. Combine lemon juice, lemon zest, garlic, salt, and pepper in a food processor fitted with a steel blade or in a blender. Puree until smooth, then, with the motor running, add olive oil in a thin stream to create an emulsified dressing. Scrape dressing into a mixing bowl, and stir in oregano and parsley.

4. Pour ½ of dressing into a heavy resealable plastic bag, and add shrimp. Allow shrimp to marinate at room temperature for 10–15 minutes, turning the bag occasionally.

5. Grill shrimp, covered, for 3–4 minutes per side, or until cooked through and opaque in the center. Serve shrimp with remaining dressing.

VARIATION: *The same marinade works beautifully with large sea scallops or with fish fillets that are at least ⅔ inch thick. The cooking time will remain the same.*

Note: The dressing can be prepared up to 1 day in advance and refrigerated, tightly covered.

Chapter 7

Poultry

Famed nineteenth-century French gastronome Jean Anthelme Brillat-Savarin once wrote that "poultry is for the cook what canvas is for the painter." Its inherently mild flavor takes to myriad methods of seasoning, and it is relatively quick to cook, too.

Almost every permutation of chicken is now available in most supermarkets—from whole birds of various sizes to delicate breast tenderloins. However, there are times and reasons why knowing how to do some chicken cutting is advantageous, so here is a brief guide:

- **Pounding chicken breasts.** Some recipes will tell you to pound the breast to an even thickness so it will cook evenly and quickly. To do so, place the breast between 2 sheets of plastic wrap , and pound with the smooth side of a meat mallet or the bottom of a small, heavy skillet or saucepan.

- **Butterflying a whole chicken.** Butterflying is a process of partially boning a whole chicken so that it can be pressed down flat on the grill and will cook over direct heat, and therefore, in less time than if you kept it whole. Turn the chicken with the breast side down, and using poultry shears cut away the backbone from the tail to the head end on both sides, and discard the backbone (or save it for making stock). Open the bird by pulling the halves apart. Use a sharp paring knife to lightly score the top of the breast bone, then run your thumbs along and under the breast bone, and pull it out. Spread the bird flat. Next turn the chicken over. Cut off the wing tips, and you are ready to grill.

Ham and Cheese-Stuffed Chicken

4 (10-ounce) chicken breast halves with skin and bones

Salt and freshly ground black pepper to taste

¼ pound Gruyère cheese, grated

¼ pound cooked ham, cut into ¼-inch dice

1 tablespoon fresh thyme or 1 teaspoon dried

3 tablespoons unsalted butter, melted

2 tablespoons freshly squeezed lemon juice

2 tablespoons Worcestershire sauce

Ham-and-Cheese-Stuffed Chicken

Yield: 4 servings | Active time: 15 minutes | Start to finish: 55 minutes

1. Prepare a medium-hot grill according to the instructions given in Chapter 1.

2. Rinse chicken and pat dry with paper towels. Insert a sharp paring knife into the thicker side of chicken breasts and cut a lengthwise pocket, being careful not to puncture the skin. Sprinkle chicken with salt and pepper, and set aside.

3. Combine cheese, ham, and thyme in a small bowl. Gently stuff mixture into pocket of chicken, and secure opening with a wooden toothpick or metal skewer. Combine butter, lemon juice, and Worcestershire sauce in a small bowl, and set aside.

4. Grill chicken, covered, for 10–12 minutes per side, basting it frequently with sauce. Do not baste for final 2 minutes of cooking, and discard any unused sauce. Chicken is cooked when it registers 160°F on an instant-read thermometer inserted into the thickest part. Serve immediately.

VARIATION: *Cheddar cheese and cooked sausage can be substituted for the Gruyère and ham, and either stuffing can also be used for pork chops.*

42

Grilled Chicken Hash

Yield: 6–8 servings | Active time: 25 minutes | Start to finish: 1 hour

1. Prepare a hot grill according to the instructions given in Chapter 1.

2. Place chicken breasts between 2 sheets of plastic wrap, and pound to an even thickness of ½ inch. Place 3 tablespoons olive oil in a mixing bowl, and add garlic, herbes de Provence, salt, and pepper. Mix well. Add chicken breasts, and stir to coat them with mixture.

3. Grill chicken for 2–3 minutes per side, uncovered, or until chicken is cooked through and no longer pink. Cut into ½-inch dice, and set aside.

4. Heat butter and remaining olive oil in a large skillet over low heat. Add onions, toss to coat with fat, and cover the pan. Cook over low heat for 10 minutes, stirring occasionally. Uncover the pan, raise the heat to medium-high, sprinkle with salt, and stir in sugar. Cook for 20–30 minutes, stirring frequently, until onions are medium brown. If onions stick to the pan, stir to incorporate browned juices into onions.

5. While onions cook, place potatoes in a saucepan and cover with cold water. Salt water and bring potatoes to a boil over high heat. Boil for 12–15 minutes, or until very tender when tested with a knife. Drain potatoes, and mash them roughly with a potato masher. Add chicken and onions to potatoes and mix well. Season to taste with salt and pepper.

6. Preheat the oven to 450°F. Spread hash into a greased 9 x 13-inch baking pan and bake for 15 minutes, or until the top is lightly brown. Serve immediately.

Note: The hash can be prepared 2 days in advance and refrigerated, tightly covered. Reheat it, covered with aluminum foil, for 10 minutes, then remove the foil and bake for an additional 15 minutes.

---

4 (6-ounce) boneless, skinless chicken breast halves

⅓ cup olive oil, divided

3 garlic cloves, peeled and minced

1 tablespoon herbes de Provence

Salt and freshly ground black pepper to taste

4 tablespoons (½ stick) unsalted butter

2 large sweet onions, such as Vidalia or Bermuda, peeled and diced

1 teaspoon granulated sugar

1½ pounds small redskin potatoes, scrubbed and quartered

4–6 (6-ounce) boneless, skinless chicken breast halves

3 tablespoons freshly squeezed lemon juice

2 garlic cloves, peeled and minced

1 tablespoon dried oregano

Salt and freshly ground black pepper to taste

⅓ cup extra-virgin olive oil, divided

1 pint cherry tomatoes, rinsed, stemmed, and chopped

½ cup pitted kalamata olives, chopped

2 tablespoons white wine vinegar

¾ cup crumbled feta cheese

Greek Chicken Paillards with Kalamata Relish

Yield: 4–6 servings | Active time: 20 minutes | Start to finish: 35 minutes

1. Prepare a hot grill according to the instructions given in Chapter 1.

2. Place chicken breasts between 2 sheets of plastic wrap, and pound to an even thickness of ½ inch. Combine lemon juice, garlic, oregano, salt, and pepper in a heavy resealable plastic bag, and mix well. Add 3 tablespoons of olive oil, and mix well again. Add chicken, and marinate at room temperature for 20 minutes, turning the bag occasionally.

3. While chicken marinates, prepare relish. Combine tomatoes, olives, remaining olive oil, and vinegar in a bowl. Season to taste with salt and pepper, and mix well. Add feta, and mix gently. Set aside.

4. Remove chicken from marinade, and discard marinade. Grill chicken for 2–3 minutes per side, uncovered, or until chicken is cooked through and no longer pink. Serve immediately, topping each chicken breast with some of the relish.

Note: The relish can be prepared up to 4 hours in advance and refrigerated, tightly covered.

4–6 (6-ounce) boneless, skinless chicken breast halves

Salt and freshly ground black pepper to taste

2 cups chopped rhubarb stalks

½ cup freshly squeezed orange juice

½ cup dry white wine

1 cup granulated sugar

3 tablespoons Dijon mustard

1 tablespoon grated orange zest

Rhubarb Chicken

Yield: 4–6 servings | Active time: 15 minutes | Start to finish: 35 minutes

1. Prepare a medium-hot grill according to the instructions given in Chapter 1. Place chicken breasts between 2 sheets of plastic wrap and pound to an even thickness of ½ inch. Sprinkle chicken with salt and pepper, and set aside.

2. Combine rhubarb, orange juice, wine, sugar, mustard, and orange zest in a heavy 2-quart saucepan, and stir well. Bring to a boil over medium-high heat, stirring occasionally. Reduce the heat to low, and simmer for 12–15 minutes, or until rhubarb is tender. Transfer ⅔ cup of mixture to a blender or food processor fitted with a steel blade, and puree until smooth.

3. Grill chicken for 2–3 minutes per side, uncovered, or until chicken is cooked through and no longer pink. Baste with pureed sauce for last 2 minutes per side of grilling. Serve immediately, passing chunky rhubarb sauce separately.

Note: Sauce can be prepared up to 1 day in advance and refrigerated, tightly covered. Allow it to reach room temperature before serving.

Thai Marinated Chicken

Yield: 4–6 servings | Active time: 25 minutes | Start to finish: 4½ hours, including 4 hours for marinating

1. Rinse chicken and pat dry with paper towels. Remove woody stalks from lemongrass, trim root end, and discard tough outer leaves; slice bulbs.

2. Combine lemongrass, cilantro, shallots, garlic, ginger, brown sugar, curry powder, fish sauce, 1 cup coconut milk, salt, and pepper in a food processor fitted with a steel blade or in a blender. Puree until smooth.

3. Pour marinade into a heavy resealable plastic bag and add chicken pieces. Marinate chicken, refrigerated, for 4 hours, or up to 24 hours, turning the bag occasionally.

4. Prepare a medium-hot grill according to the instructions given in Chapter 1.

5. Remove chicken from marinade, and transfer marinade to a small saucepan. Add reserved coconut milk, and bring to a boil over medium heat, stirring occasionally. Reduce the heat to low, and simmer sauce for 10 minutes. Season sauce to taste with salt and pepper. Strain sauce into serving bowl, and keep warm.

6. Grill chicken over a medium fire for 12 minutes per side or until white meat registers 160°F and dark meat registers 180°F on an instant-read thermometer. Serve immediately, passing sauce separately.

Note: The sauce can be made up to 4 hours in advance and refrigerated, tightly covered. This is possible if the marinade is drained from the chicken at the earlier time.

Ingredients:

- 4–6 chicken parts of your choice (breasts, thighs, legs) with bones and skin
- 4 stalks fresh lemongrass
- 1 bunch cilantro, rinsed with stems discarded
- 4 shallots, peeled and halved
- 6 garlic cloves, peeled
- 1 (2-inch) piece fresh ginger, peeled and sliced
- ¼ cup firmly packed light brown sugar
- 2 tablespoons curry powder
- ¼ cup Asian fish sauce (nam pla) *
- 1 (14.5-ounce) can unsweetened coconut milk, divided
- Salt and freshly ground black pepper to taste

* Available in the Asian aisle of most supermarkets and in specialty markets.

Middle Eastern Chicken

Yield: 4–6 servings | Active time: 10 minutes | Start to finish: 4¾ hours, including 4 hours for marinating

1. Rinse chicken and pat dry with paper towels. Combine vinegar, onion, garlic, parsley, cumin, coriander, sugar, cinnamon, cayenne, and salt in a heavy resealable plastic bag. Mix well, add olive oil, and mix well again. Add chicken and marinate, refrigerated, for a minimum of 4 hours, turning the bag occasionally.

2. Prepare a medium-hot grill according to the instructions given in Chapter 1.

3. Remove chicken from marinade, and discard marinade. Grill chicken, covered, for 12 minutes per side or until white meat registers 160°F and dark meat registers 180°F on an instant-read thermometer. Serve immediately.

VARIATION: *Pork chops can be substituted for the chicken pieces. Consult a similar recipe to determine the cooking time.*

Ingredients:

- 4–6 chicken pieces (breasts, thighs, legs) with bones and skin
- ¼ cup balsamic vinegar
- 1 small onion, peeled and chopped
- 3 garlic cloves, peeled and minced
- ¼ cup chopped fresh parsley
- 3 tablespoons ground cumin
- 2 tablespoons ground coriander
- 1 tablespoon granulated sugar
- 1 teaspoon ground cinnamon
- ½ teaspoon cayenne or to taste
- Salt to taste
- ¾ cup olive oil

2 (3-pound) whole chickens

4 bricks, wrapped in heavy-duty aluminum foil

1 stick (¼ pound) unsalted butter, softened

3 tablespoons chopped fresh parsley

2 tablespoons chopped fresh rosemary or 2 teaspoons dried

1 tablespoon fresh thyme or 1 teaspoon dried

1 tablespoon grated lemon zest

Salt and freshly ground black pepper to taste

½ lemon, seeded and very thinly sliced

Butterflied Lemon Herb Chicken

Yield: 4–6 servings | Active time: 20 minutes | Start to finish: 50 minutes

1. Rinse chickens and pat dry with paper towels. Butterfly chickens according to the instructions given above.

2. Prepare a medium-hot grill according to the instructions given in Chapter 1. Wrap 4 bricks with aluminum foil.

3. Combine butter, parsley, rosemary, thyme, lemon zest, salt, and pepper in a mixing bowl, and mix well. Stuff mixture under the skin of each chicken, being careful not to tear the skin. Lay lemon slices on top of butter mixture.

4. Place chickens over a medium fire, skin side down. Place 2 bricks on top of each chicken. Grill chicken, covered, for 10 minutes. Remove bricks, and turn chickens over. Replace bricks, and cook for an additional 12 minutes or until an instant-read thermometer registers 180°F when inserted into the thigh. Allow chickens to rest for 5 minutes, then cut into serving pieces, and serve immediately.

VARIATION: *Rather than using a whole chicken, you can make this dish with the individual parts of your choice. Consult a similar recipe to determine the cooking time.*

Butterflied Lemon Herb Chicken

Turkey Cutlets Ensalata

Yield: 6–8 servings | Active time: 15 minutes | Start to finish: 35 minutes

1. Prepare a hot grill according to the instructions given in Chapter 1.

2. Rinse turkey and pat dry with paper towels. Rub cutlets with 1 tablespoon olive oil, and sprinkle with Italian seasoning, salt, and pepper. Set aside. Combine vinegar, garlic, oregano, salt, and pepper in a jar with a tight-fitting lid, and shake well. Add remaining olive oil, and shake well again.

3. Grill turkey for 2–3 minutes per side, uncovered, or until turkey is cooked through and no longer pink. Remove turkey from the grill, and keep warm.

4. Combine tomatoes, radicchio, and scallions in a mixing bowl. Toss with dressing. To serve, top each cutlet with a portion of salad mixture, and serve immediately.

Note: The dressing can be prepared up to 1 day in advance and refrigerated, tightly covered. Allow it to reach room temperature before using.

6–8 turkey breast cutlets, about ½ inch thick

¼ cup olive oil, divided

2 teaspoons Italian seasoning

Salt and freshly ground black pepper to taste

¼ cup balsamic vinegar

2 garlic cloves, peeled and minced

1 tablespoon chopped fresh oregano or 1 teaspoon dried

1½ cups chopped fresh plum tomatoes

1 cup finely chopped radicchio

2 scallions, white parts only, rinsed, trimmed, and chopped

Asian Duck Breast

Yield: 4 servings | Active time: 20 minutes | Start to finish: 8½ hours, including 8 hours for marinating

1. Rinse duck breasts and pat dry with paper towels. Trim off all extra skin that is not covering meat, and score the remaining skin with a paring knife in a small diamond pattern, being careful not to cut into the flesh beneath the skin. Combine hoisin sauce, mirin, chile paste, cilantro, scallions, garlic, ginger, salt, and pepper in a heavy resealable plastic bag, and mix well. Add duck breasts, and mix well again to coat all surfaces. Marinate duck, refrigerated, for a minimum of 8 hours or overnight, turning the bag occasionally.

2. Prepare a medium-hot grill according to the instructions given in Chapter 1.

3. Grill duck breasts skin side down, uncovered if using a charcoal grill, for 5 minutes, or until skin is browned. Turn duck gently with tongs, and grill other side for 4–6 minutes. Remove duck from grill, and allow it to rest for 5 minutes, lightly covered with aluminum foil. Slice each breast into ½-inch slices on the diagonal, and serve immediately.

4 (7-ounce) duck breast halves

1 cup hoisin sauce *

½ cup mirin* or sherry

1 tablespoon Chinese chile paste with garlic *

¼ cup chopped cilantro

¼ cup chopped scallions

3 garlic cloves, peeled and minced

2 tablespoons grated fresh ginger

Salt and freshly ground black pepper to taste

* Available in the Asian aisle of most supermarkets and in specialty markets.

Chapter 8

Beef and Venison

Of course, there is a chapter in this book about cooking beef. After all, steaks on the grill are part and parcel of life if you list yourself amongst the ranks of carnivores. Even on a gas grill, the aroma and flavor of a grilled steak is unsurpassed.

4–6 (10-ounce) boneless rib eye, New York strip, or filet mignon steaks

Salt and freshly ground black pepper to taste

3 tablespoons unsalted butter

2 garlic cloves, peeled and minced

1 large shallot, peeled and minced

¾ cup beef stock

¾ cup dry red wine

2 tablespoons chopped fresh parsley

1 tablespoon fresh thyme or 1 teaspoon dried

⅔ cup coarsely crumbled Maytag blue cheese

½ cup panko breadcrumbs, divided

2 tablespoons vegetable oil

Steak with Maytag Blue Cheese and Red Wine Sauce

Yield: 4–6 servings | Active time: 15 minutes | Start to finish: 45 minutes

1. Prepare a dual-temperature hot-and-medium grill according to the instructions given in Chapter 1. Season both sides of the steaks with salt and pepper to taste.

2. Melt butter in a small saucepan over medium-high heat. Add garlic and shallot, and cook, stirring frequently, for 3 minutes, or until shallot is translucent. Add stock, wine, parsley, and thyme, and bring to a boil. Cook sauce until reduced by ⅔, season to taste with salt and pepper, and keep warm.

3. While sauce simmers, combine cheese and ¼ cup panko in a small bowl. Form mixture into 4–6 small discs. Press discs with remaining panko to coat evenly. Refrigerate until ready to use.

4. Sear steaks over the hot side of the grill for 2–3 minutes per side, uncovered if using a charcoal grill. Transfer steaks to the cooler side of the grill and cook for an additional 5–7 minutes, uncovered if using a charcoal grill, or to desired doneness. Allow steaks to rest for 5 minutes.

5. While steaks rest, heat oil in a small skillet over medium-high heat. Add cheese discs, and cook for 30 seconds per side, turning gently with a spatula. To serve, place steaks on plates and top each with 1 cheese disc and some sauce. Serve immediately.

Note: The sauce and cheese discs can be prepared up to 1 day in advance and refrigerated, tightly covered. Reheat sauce over low heat before using.

Korean Steak

Yield: 4–6 servings | Active time: 15 minutes | Start to finish: 3½ hours, including 3 hours for marinating

1. Rinse steaks and pat dry with paper towels. Combine ¾ cup soy sauce, sherry, sugar, 4 garlic cloves, 1 tablespoon sesame oil, and red pepper flakes in a heavy resealable plastic bag. Mix well, and add steaks. Marinate steaks, refrigerated, for a minimum of 3 hours, turning the bag occasionally.

2. Prepare a dual-temperature hot-and-medium grill according to the instructions given in Chapter 1. Combine remaining ¼ cup soy sauce, remaining 3 garlic cloves, remaining 1 tablespoon sesame oil, cilantro, vegetable oil, lime juice, and chile in a food processor fitted with a steel blade or in a blender. Puree until smooth, and set aside.

3. Sear steaks over the hot side of the grill for 2–3 minutes per side, uncovered if using a charcoal grill. Transfer steaks to the cooler side of the grill and cook for an additional 5–7 minutes, uncovered if using a charcoal grill, or to desired doneness. Allow steaks to rest for 5 minutes. To serve, slice steaks into ¾-inch slices and top with sauce. Serve immediately.

VARIATION: *Thick pork chops can be substituted for the beef steaks. Cook them to an internal temperature of 150°F.*

Note: The marinade and sauce can be prepared up to 1 day in advance and refrigerated, tightly covered. Allow them to reach room temperature before using.

4–6 (10-ounce) New York strip or boneless rib eye steaks

1 cup soy sauce, divided

¼ cup sweet sherry

3 tablespoons granulated sugar

7 garlic cloves, peeled and minced, divided

2 tablespoons Asian sesame oil,* divided

1 teaspoon red pepper flakes or to taste

½ cup firmly packed cilantro leaves

⅓ cup vegetable oil

2 tablespoons freshly squeezed lime juice

½ jalapeño or serrano chile, rinsed, seeds and ribs removed, and diced

* Available in the Asian aisle of most supermarkets and in specialty markets.

Korean Steak

4–6 (10-ounce) New York strip or boneless rib eye steaks

Salt and freshly ground black pepper to taste

¼ cup Worcestershire sauce

1 tablespoon red wine vinegar

1 tablespoon Dijon mustard

2 large shallots, peeled and minced

2 garlic cloves, peeled and minced

3 tablespoons chopped fresh parsley

2 tablespoons chopped fresh oregano or 2 teaspoons dried

1 tablespoon chopped fresh rosemary or 1 teaspoon dried

1 tablespoon fresh thyme or 1 teaspoon dried

⅓ cup extra-virgin olive oil

Steak with Herb Sauce

Yield: 4–6 servings | Active time: 25 minutes | Start to finish: 40 minutes

1. Prepare a dual-temperature hot-and-medium grill according to the instructions given in Chapter 1. Rinse steaks and pat dry with paper towels. Sprinkle steaks with salt and pepper.

2. Combine Worcestershire sauce, vinegar, mustard, shallots, garlic, parsley, oregano, rosemary, thyme, salt, and pepper in a jar with a tight-fitting lid, and shake well. Add olive oil, and shake well again. Set aside.

3. Sear steaks over the hot side of the grill for 2–3 minutes per side, uncovered if using a charcoal grill. Transfer steaks to the cooler side of the grill and cook for an additional 5–7 minutes, uncovered if using a charcoal grill, or to desired doneness. Allow steaks to rest for 5 minutes. To serve, slice steaks into ¾-inch slices and top with sauce. Serve immediately.

Note: The sauce can be prepared up to 1 day in advance and refrigerated, tightly covered. Allow it to reach room temperature before using.

2 (2-pound) T-bone or Porterhouse steaks, about 2 inches thick

¼ cup olive oil

5 garlic cloves, peeled and minced

2 tablespoons chopped fresh rosemary or 2 teaspoons dried

Salt and freshly ground black pepper to taste

4 tablespoons (½ stick) unsalted butter, softened

¼ cup freshly grated Parmesan cheese

1 tablespoon Spanish smoked paprika

2 teaspoons Dijon mustard

Steak with Tuscan Parmesan Butter

Yield: 4–6 servings | Active time: 20 minutes | Start to finish: 45 minutes

1. Prepare a dual-temperature hot-and-medium grill according to the instructions given in Chapter 1. Rinse steaks and pat dry with paper towels.

2. Combine olive oil, garlic, rosemary, salt, and pepper in a small bowl, and mix well. Rub mixture on both sides of steaks, and set aside.

3. Combine butter, Parmesan, paprika, mustard, salt, and pepper in another small bowl, and mix well. Form mixture into a log with a sheet of plastic wrap, and chill until ready to use.

4. Sear steaks over the hot side of the grill for 2–3 minutes per side, uncovered if using a charcoal grill. Transfer steaks to the cooler side of the grill and cook, uncovered if using a charcoal grill, for an additional 6–8 minutes for rare, or to desired doneness. Allow steaks to rest for 5 minutes. To serve, slice steaks into ¾-inch slices and top each serving with 1 pat of seasoned butter. Serve immediately.

Note: The butter topping can be prepared up to 1 day in advance and refrigerated, tightly covered.

Steak with Marsala Mushroom Sauce

Yield: 4–6 servings | Active time: 20 minutes | Start to finish: 45 minutes

1. Prepare a dual-temperature hot-and-medium grill according to the instructions given in Chapter 1. Rinse steaks and pat dry with paper towels. Sprinkle steaks with salt and pepper.

2. Heat oil and butter in a large skillet over medium-high heat. Add shallots and garlic and cook, stirring frequently, for 3 minutes, or until shallots are translucent. Add mushrooms and cook, stirring frequently, for 5 minutes. Add marsala, stock, parsley, and thyme. Bring to a boil, and cook, stirring occasionally, until sauce is reduced by ⅔. Season to taste with salt and pepper, and keep warm.

3. Sear steaks over the hot side of the grill for 2–3 minutes per side, uncovered if using a charcoal grill. Transfer steaks to the cooler side of the grill and cook for an additional 5–7 minutes, uncovered if using a charcoal grill, or to desired doneness. Allow steaks to rest for 5 minutes. To serve, slice steaks into ¾-inch slices and top with sauce. Serve immediately.

VARIATION: *Veal loin chops are also delicious with this sauce, as are chicken breasts.*

Note: The sauce can be prepared up to 1 day in advance and refrigerated, tightly covered. Reheat it over low heat before using.

4–6 (10-ounce) New York strip or boneless rib eye steaks

Salt and freshly ground black pepper to taste

¼ cup olive oil

3 tablespoons unsalted butter

3 shallots, peeled and minced

3 garlic cloves, peeled and minced

¾ pound mushrooms, wiped with a damp paper towel, trimmed, and sliced

1½ cups marsala wine

½ cup beef stock

¼ cup chopped fresh parsley

1 tablespoon fresh thyme or 1 teaspoon dried

Steak with Marsala Mushroom Sauce

1 (2-pound) flank steak

¼ cup soy sauce

¼ cup dry red wine

1 tablespoon Dijon
   mustard

2 tablespoons chopped
   fresh basil, preferably
   Thai basil, or 2 teaspoons
   dried

6 garlic cloves, peeled and
   minced

2 tablespoons chopped
   fresh cilantro

½ teaspoon crushed red
   pepper flakes or to taste

Salt to taste

¼ cup olive oil

Garlicky Flank Steak

Yield: 4–6 servings | Active time: 15 minutes | Start to finish: 3½ hours, including 3 hours for marinating

1. Rinse flank steak and pat dry with paper towels. Score steak lightly on both sides with a paring knife in a diamond pattern ¼-inch deep. Combine soy sauce, wine, mustard, basil, garlic, cilantro, red pepper flakes, and salt in a heavy resealable plastic bag. Mix well, add olive oil, and mix well again. Add steak to marinade and marinate, refrigerated, for a minimum of 3 hours and up to 8 hours, turning the bag occasionally.

2. Prepare a hot grill according to the instructions given in Chapter 1.

3. Grill steak, uncovered if using a charcoal grill, for 3–4 minutes per side for medium-rare, or to desired doneness. Allow steak to rest for 5 minutes, then carve into slices. Serve immediately.

Note: The marinade can be prepared up to 1 day in advance and refrigerated, tightly covered.

Garlicky Flank Steak

Steak, Potato, and Mushroom Kebabs

Yield: 4–6 servings | Active time: 25 minutes | Start to finish: 3 hours, including 2 hours for marinating

1. Soak bamboo skewers in warm water to cover. Rinse beef and pat dry with paper towels. Cut beef into 1½-inch cubes. Remove and discard mushroom stems. Wipe mushrooms clean with a damp paper towel. Cut each mushroom into 8 chunks.

2. Combine wine, vinegar, garlic, rosemary, thyme, salt, and pepper in a heavy resealable plastic bag, and mix well. Add olive oil, and mix well again. Add beef and mushrooms to the bag, and marinate, refrigerated, for 2 hours or up to 4 hours, turning the bag occasionally.

3. Place potatoes in a saucepan of salted water. Bring to a boil over high heat, and boil potatoes for 10 minutes, or until barely tender. Drain potatoes, and plunge into ice water to stop the cooking action. When cool enough to handle, cut potatoes in half, or quarter them if larger than 3 inches in diameter. Set aside.

4. Prepare a dual-temperature hot-and-medium grill according to the instructions given in Chapter 1.

5. Remove meat and mushrooms from marinade, and discard marinade. Thread beef, mushroom sections, and potatoes onto 2 parallel skewers.

6. Sear kebabs on the hot side of the grill for 1½ minutes, turning them in quarter turns, uncovered if using a charcoal grill, on the hot side of the grill. Then transfer skewers to cooler side of the grill, and cook for a total of 6 minutes more for medium-rare, or to desired doneness. Serve immediately.

VARIATION: *Cubes of boneless leg of lamb are also delicious with this recipe.*

Note: The marinade can be prepared and the potatoes can be boiled 1 day in advance and refrigerated, tightly covered.

8–12 (8-inch) bamboo skewers

2 pounds sirloin tips

2 large portobello mushrooms

¾ cup dry red wine

¼ cup balsamic vinegar

2 garlic cloves, peeled and minced

3 tablespoons chopped fresh rosemary or 1 tablespoon dried

1 tablespoon fresh thyme or 1 teaspoon dried

Salt and freshly ground black pepper to taste

⅓ cup olive oil

1 pound small new potatoes, scrubbed

4–6 (6-ounce) boneless venison steaks, cut from the loin

3 cups dry red wine, divided

2 shallots, peeled and chopped

2 garlic cloves, peeled and minced

2 tablespoons chopped fresh parsley

1 tablespoon fresh thyme or 1 teaspoon dried

2 bay leaves

Salt and freshly ground black pepper to taste

½ cup olive oil

4 tablespoons (½ stick) unsalted butter, divided

2 tablespoons vegetable oil

6 scallions, white parts only, rinsed, trimmed, and chopped

2 tablespoons brandy

Venison Steaks with Red Wine Sauce

Yield: 4–6 servings | Active time: 20 minutes | Start to finish: 8½ hours, including 8 hours for marinating

1. Rinse venison and pat dry with paper towels. Place venison between 2 sheets of plastic wrap and pound to an even thickness of ⅓ inch. Combine 1½ cups wine, shallots, garlic, parsley, thyme, bay leaves, salt, and pepper in a heavy resealable plastic bag, and mix well. Add olive oil, and mix well again. Add venison, and marinate, refrigerated, for at least 8 hours or up to 24 hours, turning the bag occasionally.

2. Prepare a hot grill according to the instructions given in Chapter 1.

3. Heat 2 tablespoons butter and vegetable oil in a saucepan over medium-high heat. Add scallions and cook, stirring frequently, for 2 minutes, or until scallions are translucent. Raise the heat to high, and add remaining 1½ cups wine and brandy. Reduce over high heat, stirring occasionally, until only ⅔ cup remains. Cut remaining butter into small pieces, and whisk butter into sauce. Season to taste with salt and pepper, and set aside.

4. Remove venison from marinade and discard marinade. Sear venison for 2–3 minutes per side, uncovered if using a charcoal grill. Top steaks with sauce, and serve immediately.

Note: The sauce can be prepared up to 1 day in advance and refrigerated, tightly covered. Reheat it over low heat before using.

Chapter 9

Lamb, Pork, and Veal

During the mid-twentieth century, when I was first exposed to fine dining, the white-tablecloth restaurants in this country were termed "continental," and one of the dishes of note was always shish kebab; sometimes it even arrived on swords rather than skewers. It was one of the few ways that many Americans enjoyed eating lamb. The same menu would frequently include some Italian veal dishes, although most likely covered in cheese, and little pork other than the occasional ham steak topped with a ring of canned pineapple.

But all of that has changed, and while beef will probably always remain the king of red meats, lamb is now growing in popularity due to its rich, rosy flavor. And both pork and veal are now dubbed "the other white meats," and are flavorful and tender alternatives to chicken.

In this chapter you will find recipes for all of these, and there are a few techniques you should know. Here are the two main ones:

- **Butterflying a leg of lamb.** It is now rather easy to find a boneless leg of lamb, but to grill successfully it has to lie much flatter on the grill. Remove the netting encasing it or cut the strings creating its cylindrical shape. Roll out the meat, and you will have parts of various thicknesses ranging from almost no meat to an area about 6 inches thick. Start by cutting away large areas of fat, and trim the solid fat coating, called the fell, on what would have been the top of the leg to an even thickness of ¼ inch. Holding your knife parallel to the counter, start slicing the thicker areas of the lamb, pulling them open as if you were rolling out a sheet of pie crust. When all the meat is basically flat, cover the lamb with a sheet of plastic wrap, and pound it to an even thickness of 2 inches with the bottom of a small skillet.

- **Trimming a pork tenderloin.** Pork tenderloins usually come in packages of two, each weighing between ¾ pound and 1 pound. The first task is to use the blade of a paring knife to scrape away the fat and very thin membrane coating the entire tenderloin. After this is accomplished you will see a stripe of iridescent white running from about halfway up the tenderloin to the thick end; this is the silver skin, and it should be removed so that the tenderloin will cook without curling. It is also very tough and gristly if eaten. Hold the end of the silver skin at the thin end with one hand, and insert a paring knife under it. Scrape it away from the meat, and repeat the process until all the silver skin has been removed.

2 pounds uncooked sausages, such as bratwurst or sweet Italian sausage

1 onion, peeled and thinly sliced

3 cups lager beer

2 tablespoons vegetable oil

Grainy mustard

Beer-Simmered Sausages

Yield: 4–6 servings | Active time: 15 minutes | Start to finish: 40 minutes

1. Prepare a medium-hot grill according to the instructions given in Chapter 1.

2. Prick sausages all over with the tip of a metal or bamboo skewer. Arrange onion slices on the bottom of a large, heavy skillet, and arrange sausages on top of onion. Add beer to cover, and bring to a boil over medium heat, covered.

3. Cook sausages for 5–6 minutes, or until partially cooked. Remove sausages from the pan with tongs, and drain on paper towels. Discard poaching liquid, but reserve onions.

4. Rub sausages with oil. Grill sausages, covered, for 4–6 minutes, turning them with tongs every 2 minutes, or until cooked through and casings are crisp. Serve immediately, accompanied with reserved onions and mustard.

Note: The sausages can be simmered up to 6 hours in advance. Refrigerate them, tightly covered.

2 pounds fresh kielbasa sausage

¾ cup granulated sugar

1¼ cups red wine vinegar

1 (3-inch) cinnamon stick

4 whole cloves

6 ripe purple plums

½ cup dry red wine

Salt and freshly ground black pepper to taste

Kielbasa with Fresh Plums

Yield: 4–6 servings | Active time: 20 minutes | Start to finish: 45 minutes

1. Prepare a medium-hot grill according to the instructions given in Chapter 1. Prick sausages all over with a metal or bamboo skewer, and set aside.

2. Combine sugar, vinegar, cinnamon, and cloves in a non-reactive saucepan, and bring to a boil over medium-high heat, stirring occasionally. Simmer 5 minutes, then add plums, cover the pan, and simmer plums for 15 minutes over low heat. Remove plums from the pan with a slotted spoon, reserving poaching liquid. When cool enough to handle, remove and discard stones and slice fruit. Set aside.

3. Combine wine and ⅔ cup poaching liquid in a small saucepan, and bring to a boil over medium-high heat. Cook until liquid is reduced by ½, then add sliced plums, and season to taste with salt and pepper. Keep warm.

4. Grill sausages, covered, for a total of 8–10 minutes, turning them with tongs every 2 minutes so they brown evenly. Allow sausages to rest for 3 minutes, then serve topped with plum sauce.

Note: The plum sauce can be prepared up to 2 days in advance and refrigerated, tightly covered. Reheat it over low heat, stirring occasionally.

Pork Chops with Apple Cream Sauce

Yield: 6–8 servings | Active time: 20 minutes | Start to finish: 5 hours, including 4 hours to brine

1. Rinse pork chops, and pat dry with paper towels. Combine 2 cups apple cider or juice, water, kosher salt, brown sugar, sage, black pepper, and cinnamon in a heavy resealable plastic bag. Mix well to dissolve sugar and salt. Add pork chops and marinate for at least 4 hours or up to 2 days, refrigerated, turning the bag occasionally.

2. While chops are brining, prepare sauce. Melt butter in a medium skillet over medium heat. Add onion, and cook, stirring frequently, for 3 minutes. Add apple to the skillet, and cook for an additional 3 minutes. Add remaining ½ cup apple cider, chicken stock, brandy, mustard, and cream to the skillet, and bring to a boil, stirring occasionally. Simmer sauce, uncovered, for 10 minutes, or until volume is reduced by ⅓. Combine cornstarch and water in a small bowl, and stir well. Add mixture to sauce, and cook for an additional 2 minutes, or until lightly thickened. Season sauce with salt and white pepper, and set aside.

3. Prepare a dual-temperature hot-and-medium grill according to the instructions given in Chapter 1. Remove chops from brine, discard brine, and pat chops dry with paper towels.

4. Grill chops, uncovered if using a charcoal grill, on the hot side of the grill for 2–3 minutes per side, and then move them to the cooler side of the grill. Grill for an additional 5–6 minutes per side for medium. Allow chops to rest for 5 minutes, then serve immediately, passing sauce separately.

Note: The sauce can be made up to 2 days in advance and refrigerated, tightly covered. Reheat it in a saucepan over low heat, stirring occasionally.

6–8 (1-inch-thick) bone-in pork chops

2½ cups apple cider or apple juice, divided

1 cup very hot tap water

¼ cup kosher salt

¼ cup firmly packed light brown sugar

1 tablespoon dried sage

2 teaspoons freshly ground black pepper

1 teaspoon ground cinnamon

2 tablespoons unsalted butter

1 onion, peeled and diced

2 Granny Smith apples, peeled, cored, quartered, and thinly sliced

½ cup chicken stock

¼ cup applejack brandy

2 tablespoons Dijon mustard

½ cup heavy cream

2 teaspoons cornstarch

2 tablespoons cold water

Salt and freshly ground white pepper to taste

Pork Chops with Apple Cream Sauce

2 (¾-pound) pork tenderloins, trimmed of fat and silver skin as described above

½ cup light molasses

⅓ cup cider vinegar

¼ cup Dijon mustard

3 garlic cloves, peeled and minced

1 shallot, peeled and chopped

1 tablespoon dried sage

Salt and freshly ground black pepper to taste

German-Style Pork Tenderloin

Yield: 4–6 servings | Active time: 20 minutes | Start to finish: 4½ hours, including 4 hours for marinating

1. Rinse pork and pat dry with paper towels. Combine molasses, vinegar, mustard, garlic, shallot, sage, salt, and pepper in a mixing bowl and whisk well.

2. Place pork in a heavy, resealable plastic bag, and pour marinade over pork. Marinate pork, refrigerated, for a minimum of 4 hours and up to 8 hours, turning the bag occasionally.

3. Prepare a dual-temperature hot-and-medium grill according to the instructions given in Chapter 1.

4. Remove pork from marinade, and transfer marinade to a small saucepan. Bring marinade to a boil over medium-high heat, stirring occasionally. Reduce the heat to low, and simmer sauce for 5 minutes.

5. Grill pork, uncovered if using a charcoal grill, on the hot side of the grill for 2–3 minutes per side, turning it in quarter turns, and then move pork to the cooler side of the grill. Grill for an additional 5–6 minutes per side for medium. Allow pork to rest for 5 minutes, then slice pork on the diagonal into ½-inch slices, and pass sauce separately.

2 cups hickory or mesquite chips

2 racks pork spareribs (about 6½ pounds)

¼ cup Aromatic Herb and Spice Rub (recipe on page 9) or any spice rub of your choice

2 cups My Favorite Barbecue Sauce (recipe on page 16) or any barbecue sauce of your choice

Basic All-American Barbecued Ribs

Yield: 4–6 servings | Active time: 20 minutes | Start to finish: 4 hours

1. If using a charcoal grill, soak hickory or mesquite chips in water for 30 minutes. If using a gas grill, create a packet for wood chips as described in Chapter 1. Rinse ribs, and pat dry with paper towels. Cut each slab in half. Rub both sides of ribs with spice rub, and allow to sit at room temperature while the grill heats.

2. Prepare a grill for indirect cooking as described in Chapter 1, pushing the coals to one side rather than around the periphery if using a charcoal grill, and lighting the burners on only one side if using a gas grill.

3. Drain wood chips and sprinkle on coals, or place packet of wood chips under grate on burners. Place ribs on the cool side of the grill, and cook for 2 hours, covered, turning the slabs every 30 minutes to cook evenly. Add more charcoal to fire after 1 hour.

4. Move ribs to hot part of grill, and baste with barbecue sauce. Cook for 5–7 minutes per side, or until ribs are browned. Remove ribs from the grill, wrap slabs in heavy-duty aluminum foil, and allow them to rest for 45 minutes.

5. Reheat foil packets on the cool side of the grill, if necessary, then cut ribs into servings, and serve immediately. Pass extra sauce separately.

Note: The ribs can be prepared up to 2 days in advance and refrigerated, tightly covered. Reheat them, covered, in a 350°F oven for 15–20 minutes, or until heated through. Uncover them for the last 5 minutes.

Basic All-American Barbecued Ribs

2 cups hickory chips

2 racks pork spareribs (about 6½ pounds)

½ cup firmly packed light brown sugar

⅓ cup paprika

1 tablespoon onion powder

1 teaspoon cayenne

Salt and freshly ground black pepper to taste

2 cups Kansas City BBQ Sauce (see recipe page 17)

Kansas City Ribs

Yield: 4–6 servings | Active time: 20 minutes | Start to finish: 4 hours

1. If using a charcoal grill, soak hickory chips in water for 30 minutes. If using a gas grill, create a packet for wood chips as described in Chapter 1. Prepare a grill for indirect cooking as described in Chapter 1, pushing the coals to one side rather than around the periphery if using a charcoal grill, and lighting the burners on only one side if using a gas grill.

2. Rinse ribs, and pat dry with paper towels. Cut each slab in half. Combine sugar, paprika, onion powder, cayenne, salt, and pepper in a bowl. Rub mixture on both sides of ribs, and allow ribs to sit at room temperature as the grill heats.

3. Drain wood chips and sprinkle on coals, or place packet of wood chips under grate on burners. Place ribs on the cool side of the grill, and cook for 2 hours, covered, turning the slabs every 30 minutes to cook evenly. Add more charcoal to fire after 1 hour.

4. Move ribs to hot part of grill, and baste with barbecue sauce. Cook for 5–7 minutes per side, or until ribs are browned. Remove ribs from the grill, wrap slabs in heavy-duty aluminum foil, and allow to rest for 45 minutes.

5. Reheat foil packets on the cool side of the grill, if necessary, then cut ribs into servings, and serve immediately. Pass extra sauce separately.

Note: The ribs can be prepared up to 2 days in advance and refrigerated, tightly covered. Reheat them, covered, in a 350°F oven for 15–20 minutes, or until heated through. Uncover them for the last 5 minutes.

3 pounds boneless leg of lamb, fat trimmed, and cut into 1-inch cubes

1 cup dry red wine

2 shallots, peeled and chopped

4 garlic cloves, peeled and minced

2 tablespoons dried oregano

½ teaspoon ground cinnamon

Salt and freshly ground black pepper to taste

½ cup olive oil

12–16 (8-inch) bamboo skewers

Greek Feta Sauce (see recipe page 19)

Middle Eastern Lamb Kebabs with Greek Feta Raita

Yield: 6–8 servings | Active time: 20 minutes | Start to finish: 1½ hours, including 1 hour for marinating

1. Rinse lamb, and pat dry with paper towels. Combine wine, shallots, garlic, oregano, cinnamon, salt, and pepper in a heavy, resealable plastic bag, and mix well. Add olive oil, and mix well again. Add lamb, and marinate for 1 hour at room temperature or up to 6 hours refrigerated, turning the bag occasionally.

2. Soak bamboo skewers in warm water to cover, and prepare a medium-hot grill according to the instructions given in Chapter 1.

3. Remove lamb from marinade, and discard marinade. Thread lamb onto 2 parallel skewers. Grill lamb, uncovered, for 2–3 minutes per side, turning it in quarter turns, for medium-rare. Serve immediately, passing Greek Feta Sauce separately.

Moroccan Lamb Chops

Yield: 4–6 servings | Active time: 15 minutes | Start to finish: 1¼ hours, including 1 hour for marinating

1. Rinse lamb and pat dry with paper towels. Combine olive oil, cilantro, garlic, paprika, coriander, cumin, salt, and pepper in a heavy resealable plastic bag, and mix well. Add chops, coating them well with mixture. Marinate chops at room temperature for 1 hour, turning the bag occasionally, or up to 6 hours, refrigerated.

2. Prepare a medium-hot grill according to the instructions given in Chapter 1.

3. Remove lamb chops from marinade, and discard marinade.

4. Grill chops, covered, for 3 minutes per side for medium-rare or to desired doneness. Serve immediately.

Note: The lamb chops can be grilled up to 1 day in advance and refrigerated, tightly covered. Reheat them in a single layer in a 450°F oven for 3 minutes per side, or until heated through.

2 (8-rib) racks of lamb, cut into 1-rib serving pieces

½ cup olive oil

1 cup chopped fresh cilantro

4 garlic cloves, peeled and minced

1 tablespoon paprika

1 tablespoon ground coriander

1 teaspoon ground cumin

Salt and freshly ground black pepper to taste

Moroccan Lamb Chops

6 (1-inch-thick) veal chops

⅓ cup freshly squeezed
   lemon juice

½ cup chopped fresh
   parsley, divided

¼ cup chopped fresh
   rosemary, divided

1 tablespoon fresh thyme
   or 1 teaspoon dried

3 garlic cloves, peeled and
   minced, divided

1 shallot, peeled and
   chopped

Salt and freshly ground
   black pepper to taste

½ cup olive oil

1 tablespoon grated lemon
   zest

Lemon-Herb Veal Chops

Yield: 6 servings | Active time: 15 minutes | Start to finish: 4½ hours, including 4 hours for marinating

1. Rinse veal chops and pat dry with paper towels. Combine lemon juice, ¼ cup parsley, 2 tablespoons rosemary, thyme, 2 garlic cloves, shallot, salt, and pepper in a heavy resealable plastic bag, and mix well. Add olive oil, and mix well again. Add chops and marinate, refrigerated, for 4–6 hours, turning the bag occasionally.

2. While chops marinate, combine remaining parsley, remaining rosemary, remaining garlic, and lemon zest in a small bowl. Mix well, and set aside.

3. Prepare a dual-temperature hot-and-medium grill according to the instructions given in Chapter 1.

4. Remove chops from marinade, discard marinade, and pat chops dry with paper towels. Grill chops on the hot side of the grill, uncovered if using a charcoal grill, for 3–4 minutes per side, then move them to the cooler side of the grill and cook for 4–5 minutes per side for medium or to desired doneness. Transfer chops to a platter or individual plates, and allow chops to rest for 5 minutes. Then sprinkle each with a few teaspoons of topping, and serve immediately.

VARIATION: *Thick pork chops are also delicious when soaked in this marinade.*

Chapter 10

Burgers of All Types

Seymour, Wisconsin, is one of the cities that claims the parentage of the hamburger, and dates it to the flattening of a meatball to place it between two slices of bread in 1885. Charlie Nagreen not only sold burgers on the fair circuit, he also peddled Christmas trees, popcorn, and party costumes. Seymour was so convinced of his identification as the father of the hamburger that the city boasts a yearly Burger Fest; in 1989 it made the *Guinness Book of World Records* by serving the "world's largest hamburger." It weighed more than 5,000 pounds.

Herbed Midwestern Turkey Burgers
Yield: 4–6 servings | Active time: 15 minutes | Start to finish: 40 minutes

1. Prepare a dual-temperature hot-and-medium grill according to the instructions given in Chapter 1.

2. Combine turkey with apple, sage, and allspice. Season to taste with salt and pepper. Form mixture into 4–6 (¾-inch-thick) burgers.

3. Grill rolls on the hot side of the grill, cut-side down, until toasted. Sear burgers over high heat for 2 minutes per side, uncovered if using a charcoal grill, and then transfer burgers to the cooler side of the grill. Continue to cook, covered, for 3–5 minutes per side, or until burgers register 160°F on an instant-read thermometer and are cooked through and no longer pink. Serve immediately on rolls with lettuce, tomato, and red onion.

VARIATION: *Ground pork or ground veal can be substituted for the turkey. Cook these meats to desired doneness.*

Note: The turkey mixture can be prepared up to 1 day in advance and refrigerated, tightly covered.

1¾ pounds ground turkey

1 Golden Delicious or Granny Smith apple, peeled, cored, and grated

3 tablespoons chopped fresh sage or 1 tablespoon dried

¼ teaspoon ground allspice

Salt and freshly ground black pepper to taste

4–6 rolls of your choice, sliced in half

Lettuce, tomato, and thinly sliced red onion

1 cup mayonnaise

1 cup tightly packed chopped fresh basil

¼ cup chopped fresh parsley

¼ cup small capers, drained and rinsed

2 garlic cloves, peeled and minced

1 large shallot, peeled and chopped

2 teaspoons herbes de Provence

Salt and freshly ground black pepper to taste

1¾ pounds ground turkey

4–6 rolls of your choice, sliced in half

Lettuce, tomato, and thinly sliced red onion

Turkey Burgers Provençal

Yield: 4–6 servings | Active time: 15 minutes | Start to finish: 45 minutes

1. Prepare a dual-temperature hot-and-medium grill according to the instructions given in Chapter 1.

2. Combine mayonnaise, basil, parsley, capers, garlic, shallot, herbes de Provence, salt, and pepper in a mixing bowl, and stir well.

3. Combine ½ cup mayonnaise mixture and turkey in a mixing bowl, and mix gently. Form mixture into 4–6 (¾-inch-thick) burgers.

4. Grill rolls on the hot side of the grill cut-side down until toasted. Sear burgers over high heat for 2 minutes per side, uncovered if using a charcoal grill, and then transfer burgers to the cooler side of the grill. Continue to cook, covered, for 3–5 minutes per side, or until burgers register 160°F on an instant-read thermometer and are cooked through and no longer pink.

5. Serve immediately with remaining mayonnaise mixture, lettuce, tomato, and onion.

VARIATION: *Ground pork or ground veal can be substituted for the turkey. Cook these meats to desired doneness.*

Note: The turkey mixture can be prepared up to 1 day in advance and refrigerated, tightly covered.

2 cups lentils, picked over, rinsed, and drained

1 quart water

1 teaspoon salt

¾ cup pine nuts

2 tablespoons vegetable oil

1 medium onion, peeled and chopped

2 garlic cloves, peeled and minced

2 teaspoons ground coriander

1 teaspoon ground cumin

Salt and freshly ground black pepper to taste

4–6 sesame buns, sliced in half

Lettuce, tomato, and hummus

Middle Eastern Lentil Burgers

Yield: 4–6 servings | Active time: 20 minutes | Start to finish: 40 minutes

1. Place lentils in a 2-quart saucepan, cover with water, and add 1 teaspoon salt. Bring to a boil over medium-high heat, then reduce the heat to low and simmer lentils, covered, for 20–25 minutes, or until cooked. Drain lentils, and place in a mixing bowl.

2. Prepare a medium-hot grill according to the instructions given in Chapter 1.

3. While lentils simmer, place pine nuts in a small, dry skillet over medium-high heat. Toast nuts, shaking pan frequently, for 2–3 minutes, or until browned. Remove nuts from the pan, and set aside. Heat oil in the same small skillet over medium-high heat. Add onions and garlic, and cook, stirring frequently, for 3 minutes, or until onion is translucent. Add coriander and cumin, and cook, stirring constantly, for 1 minute. Add onion mixture to lentils, and stir well.

4. Puree ½ cup pine nuts and 1 cup lentil mixture in a food processor fitted with a metal blade. Scrape mixture back into a mixing bowl, and add remaining lentil mixture and remaining pine nuts. Season to taste with salt and pepper. Form mixture into 4–6 (¾-inch-thick) burgers.

5. Grill buns cut-side down until toasted. Grill burgers for 3 minutes per side, covered, turning them gently with a spatula. Serve immediately on buns with lettuce, tomato, and hummus.

Note: The lentil mixture can be prepared up to 1 day in advance and refrigerated, tightly covered. Allow it to reach room temperature before grilling the burgers.

Dilled Salmon Burgers
Yield: 4–6 servings | Active time: 20 minutes | Start to finish: 2 hours

1 (1½-pound) salmon fillet, skinned

¼ cup Dijon mustard, divided

¼ cup chopped fresh dill, divided

Salt and freshly ground black pepper to taste

¼ cup mayonnaise

¼ cup sour cream

2 tablespoons vegetable oil

4–6 rolls of your choice, sliced in half

Lettuce, tomato, and thinly sliced red onion

1. Rinse salmon and pat dry with paper towels, and cut into 1-inch pieces. Place salmon cubes on a sheet of plastic wrap, and freeze for 20–30 minutes, or until firm but not solid. Chop salmon in a food processor fitted with a steel blade using on-and-off pulsing. Place salmon in a mixing bowl and add 2 tablespoons mustard and 2 tablespoons dill. Season to taste with salt and pepper.

2. Form salmon mixture into 4–6 (¾-inch-thick) burgers. Cover burgers with plastic wrap, and refrigerate for at least 45 minutes.

3. Prepare a medium-hot grill according to the instructions given in Chapter 1. While burgers chill, combine mayonnaise and sour cream with remaining mustard and remaining dill. Stir well, and refrigerate until ready to use.

4. Grill rolls, cut-side down, until toasted. Rub burgers with oil, and grill for 3 minutes per side, covered, for a medium-rare burger or to desired doneness. Serve immediately on rolls with sauce, lettuce, tomato, and onion slices.

VARIATION: *Tuna or a firm-fleshed white fish like cod or halibut can be substituted for the salmon.*

Note: The burgers can be formed up to 6 hours in advance and refrigerated, tightly covered.

1¾ pounds tuna fillets

3 scallions, white parts only, rinsed, trimmed, and chopped

2 garlic cloves, peeled and minced

2 tablespoons freshly grated ginger

2 tablespoons fish sauce (nam pla) *

1 tablespoon mirin* or sweet sherry

Salt and freshly ground black pepper to taste

1 tablespoon wasabi powder *

2 tablespoons cold water

⅔ cup mayonnaise

3 tablespoons finely chopped pickled ginger

2 teaspoons Asian sesame oil*

4–6 rolls of your choice, sliced in half

2 tablespoons vegetable oil

Lettuce and tomato

* Available in the Asian aisle of most supermarkets and in specialty markets.

Tuna Burgers with Wasabi Mayonnaise

Yield: 4–6 servings | Active time: 20 minutes | Start to finish: 2 hours

1. Rinse tuna and pat dry with paper towels, and cut into 1-inch pieces, discarding sinews. Place tuna cubes on a sheet of plastic wrap, and freeze for 20–30 minutes, or until firm but not solid. Chop tuna in a food processor fitted with a steel blade using on-and-off pulsing. Place tuna in a mixing bowl and add scallions, garlic, ginger, fish sauce, mirin, salt, and pepper.

2. Form tuna mixture into 4–6 (¾-inch-thick) burgers. Cover burgers with plastic wrap, and refrigerate for at least 45 minutes.

3. Prepare a hot grill according to the instructions given in Chapter 1. While burgers chill, combine wasabi and water in a mixing bowl to form a paste. Add mayonnaise, pickled ginger, and sesame oil. Stir well, and refrigerate until ready to use.

4. Grill rolls, cut-side down, until toasted. Rub burgers with oil, and grill for 2–3 minutes per side, uncovered if using a charcoal grill, for a rare burger or to desired doneness. Serve immediately on rolls with lettuce, tomato, and wasabi mayonnaise.

Note: The burgers can be formed up to 6 hours in advance and refrigerated, tightly covered.

Mexican Beef and Chorizo Burgers

Yield: 4–6 servings | Active time: 15 minutes | Start to finish: 40 minutes

1. Prepare a medium-hot grill according to the instructions given in Chapter 1.

2. Remove casings from chorizo, if necessary, and chop chorizo finely in a food processor fitted with a steel blade using on-and-off pulsing. Combine chorizo, ground chuck, shallots, 3 garlic cloves, cilantro, chili powder, cumin, and oregano in a mixing bowl. Season to taste with salt and cayenne. Mix well, and form mixture into 8–12 (⅓-inch-thick) patties. Place cheese on half of patties, and top with remaining patties. Press together gently to enclose cheese. Press with your thumb in the center of each burger to form an indentation; this keeps the burgers from creating a dome in the center.

3. Combine mayonnaise, remaining garlic, green chilies, and lime juice in a small bowl. Season with salt and cayenne to taste, and stir well. Set aside.

4. Grill rolls, cut-side down, until toasted. Grill burgers beginning with the side with the indentation up, uncovered if using a charcoal grill, for a total time of 4–6 minutes per side or to an internal temperature of 125°F for medium-rare or to desired doneness. To serve, place burgers on bottom half of rolls and top each with mayonnaise mixture. Serve immediately with lettuce, tomato, and red onion.

VARIATION: *Ground turkey can be substituted for the beef. Cook burgers to an internal temperature of 160°F on an instant-read thermometer or until cooked through and no longer pink.*

Note: The beef mixture can be prepared up to 1 day in advance and refrigerated, tightly covered.

- ½ pound chorizo
- 1 pound ground chuck
- 2 shallots, peeled and finely chopped
- 4 garlic cloves, peeled and minced, divided
- 3 tablespoons chopped fresh cilantro
- 2 tablespoons chili powder
- 2 teaspoons ground cumin
- 1 teaspoon dried oregano
- Salt and cayenne to taste
- 1 cup grated jalapeño Jack cheese
- ¾ cup mayonnaise
- 2 tablespoons diced canned mild green chiles, drained
- 1 tablespoon freshly squeezed lime juice
- 4–6 rolls of your choice, sliced in half
- Lettuce, tomato slices, and thin slices of red onion

Beef burger

1¾ pounds ground pork

12 scallions, white parts and 2 inches of green tops, rinsed, trimmed, and thinly sliced, divided

¼ cup grated fresh ginger

¼ cup chopped fresh cilantro

4 garlic cloves, peeled and minced

¼ cup soy sauce

2 tablespoons dry sherry

½ cup finely chopped water chestnuts

Freshly ground black pepper to taste

½ cup Dijon mustard

¼ cup hoisin sauce *

4–6 sesame rolls, sliced in half

Lettuce, tomato slices, and thin slices of red onion

*Available in the Asian aisle of most supermarkets and in specialty markets.

Chinese Pork Burgers

Yield: 4–6 servings | Active time: 20 minutes | Start to finish: 45 minutes

1. Prepare a medium-hot grill according to the instructions given in Chapter 1.

2. Combine pork, half of scallions, ginger, cilantro, garlic, soy sauce, sherry, water chestnuts, and pepper in a mixing bowl. Mix well and form into 4–6 (¾-inch-thick) burgers. Press with your thumb in the center of each burger to form an indentation; this keeps the burgers from creating a dome in the center. Combine mustard and hoisin sauce in a bowl, whisk well, and set aside.

3. Grill rolls, cut-side down, until toasted. Grill burgers beginning with the side with the indentation up, uncovered if using a charcoal grill, for a total time of 4–6 minutes per side or to an internal temperature of 150°F on an instant-read thermometer. Baste burgers with sauce for last 4 minutes of grilling.

4. Add remaining scallions to remaining sauce. Serve immediately on rolls with lettuce and tomato. Pass sauce separately.

VARIATION: Ground turkey or ground veal can be substituted for the pork. The turkey should be grilled to an internal temperature of 160°F or until cooked through and no longer pink.

Note: The pork mixture can be prepared up to 1 day in advance and refrigerated, tightly covered.

Chinese Pork Burgers

Greek Lamb Burgers

Yield: 4–6 servings | Active time: 20 minutes | Start to finish: 40 minutes

1. Prepare a medium-hot grill according to the instructions given in Chapter 1.

2. Place yogurt in a strainer set over a mixing bowl. Shake strainer gently a few times, and allow yogurt to drain for at least 30 minutes at room temperature, or up to 6 hours refrigerated. Discard whey from mixing bowl, and place yogurt in the bowl. Set aside.

3. Combine lamb, shallots, garlic, parsley, oregano, thyme, and cumin in a mixing bowl. Season to taste with salt and pepper. Mix well, and form mixture into 4–6 (1-inch-thick) burgers. Press with your thumb in the center of each burger to form an indentation; this keeps the burgers from creating a dome in the center.

4. Grill burgers beginning with the side with the indentation up, uncovered if using a charcoal grill, for a total time of 4–6 minutes per side or to an internal temperature of 125°F for medium-rare or to desired doneness.

5. While burgers grill, combine drained yogurt, cucumber, and tomato in a small bowl. Season to taste with salt and pepper.

6. To serve, cut top 1 inch off pita breads and place burgers inside. Split pita breads and place burgers inside. Top each with yogurt mixture, and serve immediately.

VARIATION: *Ground beef can be substituted for the ground lamb.*

Note: The lamb mixture can be prepared up to 1 day in advance and refrigerated, tightly covered.

Ingredients

- ⅔ cup plain yogurt
- 1¾ pounds ground lamb
- 2 shallots, peeled and finely chopped
- 3 garlic cloves, peeled and minced
- ¼ cup chopped fresh parsley
- 2 tablespoons chopped fresh oregano or 2 teaspoons dried
- 1 tablespoon fresh thyme or 1 teaspoon dried
- 2 teaspoons ground cumin
- Salt and freshly ground black pepper to taste
- 4–6 (8-inch) pita breads
- ½ cup finely chopped cucumber
- 2 ripe plum tomatoes, rinsed, cored, seeded, and finely chopped

Chapter 11

Entree Salads

The recipes in this chapter can be considered a "two-fer." Entree salads—loaded with healthful fresh vegetables and some grilled protein—are also a great way to use up leftover grilled food from a previous meal. Stunning when they arrive at the table, the salads in this chapter are a complete meal, perhaps with the addition of some crusty bread. So do not be put off if the preparation time seems long; the salad is all you have to create.

1 cup apple wood chips

4–6 (12-ounce) rainbow trout, scaled and gutted, with head left on

3 tablespoons olive oil

Salt and freshly ground black pepper to taste

½ cup sour cream

2 tablespoons prepared horseradish

2 tablespoons chopped fresh dill or 2 teaspoons dried

3 tablespoons freshly squeezed lemon juice

1 pint cherry tomatoes, rinsed and halved

½ English cucumber, cut into ⅓-inch dice

½ small red onion, peeled, halved lengthwise, and thinly sliced

4–6 cups chopped romaine, rinsed and dried

Rainbow Trout Salad with Horseradish Dressing

Yield: 4–6 servings | Active time: 20 minutes | Start to finish: 40 minutes

1. Prepare a medium-hot grill according to the instructions given in Chapter 1. Rinse trout and pat dry with paper towels. If using a charcoal grill, soak apple wood chips in water for 30 minutes. If using a gas grill, create a packet for wood chips as described in Chapter 1.

2. Rub fish with oil, and sprinkle with salt and pepper. Set aside. Combine sour cream, horseradish, dill, lemon juice, salt, and pepper in a bowl, and whisk well. Refrigerate until ready to use.

3. Combine tomatoes, cucumber, onion, and lettuce in a mixing bowl, and toss with enough dressing to coat vegetables lightly.

4. Grill trout for 4 minutes per side, uncovered if using a charcoal grill, or until skin is crisp and flesh is no longer translucent.

5. To serve, mound vegetable mixture onto a serving platter or individual plates, and top with trout. Serve immediately, passing extra dressing separately.

Note: The dressing can be made up to 1 day in advance and refrigerated, tightly covered.

Tuna Salad Niçoise

Yield: 4–6 servings | Active time: 20 minutes | Start to finish: 45 minutes

1. Place potatoes in a saucepan of salted water, and bring to a boil over high heat. Boil potatoes for 8–10 minutes, or until tender. Add green beans, and boil 2 minutes more. Drain vegetables, and rinse under cold running water. Refrigerate vegetables until cold.

2. Prepare a hot grill according to the instructions given in Chapter 1. Sprinkle tuna with salt and pepper, and place it on a sheet of plastic wrap in the freezer for 20–30 minutes.

3. Combine lemon juice, mustard, herbes de Provence, salt, and pepper in a jar with a tight-fitting lid, and shake well. Add olive oil, and shake well again.

4. Grill tuna steaks, uncovered if using a charcoal grill, for 2–3 minutes per side; the inside should remain almost raw, or cook to desired doneness. Slice steaks into ¼-inch slices against the grain, and set aside.

5. Toss salad greens with ¼ of dressing, and arrange on a platter or individual plates. Top greens with tuna, potatoes, and green beans, and drizzle with additional dressing. Scatter olives, tomatoes, capers, parsley, and Parmesan over all, and serve immediately, passing remaining dressing separately.

Note: The vegetables can be boiled and the dressing can be made up to 1 day in advance and refrigerated, tightly covered. Bring the dressing to room temperature before using.

- 1 pound baby new potatoes, scrubbed and quartered
- ¼ pound green beans, rinsed and stemmed
- 3 (8-ounce) fresh tuna steaks, at least ¾ inch thick
- ¼ cup freshly squeezed lemon juice
- 2 teaspoons Dijon mustard
- 1 teaspoon herbes de Provence
- Salt and freshly ground black pepper to taste
- ⅓ cup extra-virgin olive oil
- 4–6 cups mixed baby greens, rinsed and dried
- ½ cup pitted Niçoise or other oil-cured black olives, halved lengthwise
- 1 cup cherry tomatoes, rinsed and halved
- 2 tablespoons capers, drained and rinsed
- ¼ cup chopped fresh parsley leaves
- ¼ cup freshly grated Parmesan cheese

8–12 (8-inch) bamboo skewers

⅓ cup freshly squeezed lemon juice

4 garlic cloves, peeled and minced

2 tablespoons chopped fresh oregano or 2 teaspoons dried

2 tablespoons chopped fresh parsley

Salt and freshly ground black pepper to taste

½ cup extra-virgin olive oil, divided

1 pint cherry tomatoes, rinsed and halved

½ English cucumber, cut into ⅓-inch dice

½ small red onion, peeled, halved lengthwise, and thinly sliced

1½ pounds extra large (16–20 per pound) raw shrimp, peeled and deveined

1 orange or yellow bell pepper, seeds and ribs removed, and cut into ½-inch slices

4–6 cups chopped baby spinach leaves, rinsed and dried

1 cup crumbled feta cheese

1 cup pitted kalamata olives

Greek Shrimp Salad

Yield: 4–6 servings | Active time: 20 minutes | Start to finish: 40 minutes

1. Soak bamboo skewers in warm water to cover, and prepare a medium-hot grill according to the instructions given in Chapter 1.

2. Combine lemon juice, garlic, oregano, parsley, salt, and pepper in a jar with a tight-fitting lid, and shake well. Add ⅓ cup olive oil, and shake well again.

3. Place tomatoes, cucumber, and red onion in a large mixing bowl. Toss with ⅓ of dressing, and refrigerate. Place shrimp in a heavy resealable plastic bag, and add ⅓ of dressing. Seal and turn bag to coat shrimp evenly. Marinate shrimp at room temperature for 10 minutes, or up to 30 minutes refrigerated.

4. Grill pepper slices, covered, for 3–5 minutes, or until soft. Remove peppers from the grill, and slice into strips. Add peppers to bowl with other vegetables.

5. Remove shrimp from marinade, and discard marinade. Divide shrimp into 4–6 groups, and thread each group onto two parallel skewers. Grill shrimp, covered, for 2 minutes per side, or until pink and cooked through. Remove shrimp from skewers.

6. To serve, place 1 portion romaine on each plate, and top with vegetables and shrimp. Sprinkle feta and olives on top, and serve immediately, passing remaining dressing separately.

VARIATION: *Any firm white-fleshed fish fillet, such as halibut or cod, will be just as delicious as the shrimp and will cook in the same amount of time. You can also substitute ¾-inch cubes of boneless, skinless chicken breast. The chicken should be marinated, refrigerated, for 1 hour, and the pieces should be cooked for 4–6 minutes per side, or until cooked through and no longer pink.*

Note: The dressing can be made up to 1 day in advance and refrigerated, tightly covered. Bring to room temperature before using.

Greek Shrimp Salad

1½ pounds boneless, skinless chicken breasts, rinsed and patted dry with paper towels

1 cup olive oil, divided

3 garlic cloves, peeled and minced

1 tablespoon dried sage

2 teaspoons dried thyme

Salt and freshly ground black pepper to taste

3 tablespoons honey

3 tablespoons Dijon mustard

⅓ cup cider vinegar

1½ pounds baby spinach, washed and stemmed if necessary

2 carrots, peeled and thinly sliced

1 red bell pepper, seeds and ribs removed, cut into thin slices

1 red onion, peeled and cut into thin rings

Chicken and Spinach Salad

Yield: 6–8 servings | Active time: 25 minutes | Start to finish: 30 minutes

1. Prepare a hot grill according to the instructions given in Chapter 1.

2. Trim chicken breasts of all visible fat, and pound to an even thickness of ½ inch between 2 sheets of plastic wrap. Place chicken breasts in a mixing bowl, and toss with ¼ cup olive oil, garlic, sage, thyme, salt, and pepper.

3. Combine honey, mustard, vinegar, remaining ¾ cup oil, salt, and pepper in a mixing bowl, and whisk well. Set aside.

4. Grill chicken for 2–3 minutes per side, uncovered, or until chicken is cooked through and no longer pink. Remove chicken from the grill, and set aside.

5. To serve, combine spinach, carrots, bell pepper, and onion in a mixing bowl, and toss with enough dressing to coat vegetables lightly. Mound mixture onto a serving platter or individual plates, and top with chicken slices. Serve immediately, passing extra dressing separately.

VARIATION: *This salad is also excellent with grilled shrimp; consult a similar recipe for instructions on grilling the shrimp.*

Note: The dressing can be made up to 1 day in advance and refrigerated, tightly covered. Bring to room temperature before using.

Chicken and Spinach Salad

Grilled Chicken Caesar Salad

Grilled Chicken Caesar Salad

Yield: 6–8 servings | Active time: 25 minutes | Start to finish: 35 minutes

1. Prepare a hot grill according to the instructions given in Chapter 1.

2. Trim chicken breasts of all visible fat, and pound to an even thickness of ½ inch between 2 sheets of plastic wrap. Place chicken breasts in a mixing bowl.

3. To prepare dressing, bring a small saucepan of water to a boil over high heat. Add egg and boil for 1 minute. Remove egg from water with a slotted spoon and break it into a jar with a tight-fitting lid, scraping the inside of the shell. Add anchovy paste, garlic, lemon juice, and mustard, and shake well. Add ⅓ cup olive oil, and shake well again. Season to taste with pepper.

4. Reserve ½ of dressing, and mix remaining dressing into bowl with chicken breasts. Use reserved oil to brush both sides of bread.

5. Grill chicken for 2–3 minutes per side, uncovered, or until chicken is cooked through and no longer pink. Grill bread for 1–2 minutes per side, or until toasted. Remove chicken from the grill, and cut into thin slices against the grain. Remove bread from the grill, and cut into ½-inch croutons.

6. To serve, combine croutons, lettuce, and Parmesan in a mixing bowl, and toss with enough dressing to coat lightly. Mound mixture onto a serving platter or individual plates, and top with chicken slices. Serve immediately, passing extra dressing separately.

VARIATION: *Grilled shrimp or cubes of salmon can be used instead of chicken for an aquatic treat.*

Note: The dressing can be made up to 1 day in advance and refrigerated, tightly covered. Bring to room temperature before using.

1½ pounds boneless, skinless chicken breasts, rinsed and patted dry with paper towels

1 large egg

1 (2-ounce) tube anchovy paste

5 garlic cloves, minced

¼ cup freshly squeezed lemon juice

2 tablespoons Dijon mustard

½ cup extra-virgin olive oil, divided

Freshly ground black pepper to taste

6–8 (½-inch-thick) slices French or Italian bread

6–8 cups baby greens or bite-sized pieces romaine lettuce, rinsed and dried

½ cup freshly grated Parmesan cheese

6–8 anchovy fillets (optional)

1 (2-pound) flank steak

⅓ cup rice wine vinegar

3 tablespoons soy sauce

3 tablespoons Dijon mustard

2 tablespoons hoisin sauce*

3 tablespoons grated fresh ginger

4 garlic cloves, peeled and minced

2 scallions, trimmed and finely chopped

Freshly ground black pepper to taste

¾ cup vegetable oil

¼ cup Asian sesame oil*

¼ pound snow peas, tips removed

1 pound baby spinach leaves, rinsed and stemmed

¼ pound bean sprouts, rinsed

2 cucumbers, peeled, halved, and thinly sliced

1 red bell pepper, seeds and ribs removed, thinly sliced

* Available in the Asian aisle of most supermarkets and in specialty markets.

Asian Steak Salad

Yield: 6–8 servings | Active time: 25 minutes | Start to finish: 4¼ hours, including 4 hours for marinating

1. Rinse steak and pat dry with paper towels. Score steak with a paring knife on both sides in a diagonal pattern ¼-inch deep.

2. Combine vinegar, soy sauce, mustard, hoisin sauce, ginger, garlic, scallions, and black pepper in a jar with a tight-fitting lid. Shake well. Add vegetable and sesame oils and shake well again.

3. Place steak in a heavy resealable plastic bag, and add ½ cup of dressing. Marinate steak, refrigerated, for 4 hours, turning the bag occasionally.

4. While steak marinates, place snow peas in a microwave-safe container with 1 tablespoon water. Microwave on HIGH (100% power) for 30 seconds. Plunge snow peas into a bowl of ice water. Drain. Combine snow peas with spinach, bean sprouts, cucumbers, and red pepper in a salad bowl, and refrigerate.

5. Prepare a hot grill according to the instructions given in Chapter 1.

6. Grill steak for 5–7 minutes, uncovered if using a charcoal grill, or until browned. Turn meat with tongs, and grill for an additional 2–3 minutes for medium-rare, or to desired doneness. Allow steak to rest for 5 minutes, then slice it thinly on the diagonal.

7. To serve, toss salad with ⅓ cup of dressing. Mound mixture onto a serving platter or individual plates, and top with steak slices. Serve immediately, passing extra dressing separately.

VARIATION: *You can substitute slices of grilled chicken breast or fish steaks for the beef in this recipe. Consult a similar recipe for cooking instructions.*

Note: The dressing can be made up to 1 day in advance and refrigerated, tightly covered. Bring to room temperature before using.

Steak and Maytag Blue Cheese Salad

Yield: 4–6 servings | Active time: 25 minutes | Start to finish: 45 minutes

1. Prepare a dual-temperature hot-and-medium grill according to the instructions given in Chapter 1.

2. Sprinkle steaks with salt and pepper. Combine vinegar, garlic, shallot, parsley, thyme, sugar, salt, and pepper in a jar with a tight-fitting lid, and shake well. Add olive oil, and shake well again. Set aside.

3. Sear steaks on the hot side of the grill for 2–3 minutes per side, uncovered if using a charcoal grill, or until well browned. Transfer steaks to the cooler side of the grill, and cook for an additional 2–3 minutes per side for rare, when an instant-read thermometer registers 120°F. Remove steaks from the grill, and allow them to rest for 5 minutes.

4. Combine romaine, radicchio, onion, tomatoes, and blue cheese in a mixing bowl. To serve, toss salad with ⅓ cup of dressing. Mound mixture onto a serving platter or individual plates, and top with steak slices. Serve immediately, passing extra dressing separately.

Note: The dressing can be made up to 1 day in advance and refrigerated, tightly covered. Bring to room temperature before using.

1½ pounds New York strip steak or boneless rib eye steak, at least 1 inch thick

Salt and freshly ground black pepper to taste

½ cup red wine vinegar

2 garlic cloves, peeled and minced

1 shallot, peeled and minced

2 tablespoons chopped fresh parsley

1 tablespoon fresh thyme or 1 teaspoon dried

2 teaspoons granulated sugar

1 cup olive oil

4 cups bite-sized pieces romaine lettuce, rinsed and dried

1 large head radicchio, rinsed, cored, and chopped

½ small red onion, peeled and thinly sliced

½ pint cherry tomatoes, rinsed and halved

1 cup crumbled Maytag blue cheese

1 cup cracked-wheat bulgur

2 cups boiling water

1 (15-ounce) can garbanzo beans, drained and rinsed

2 large tomatoes, rinsed, cored, seeded, and diced

1 cup chopped fresh parsley

1 bunch scallions, white parts and 2 inches of green tops, rinsed, trimmed, and thinly sliced

½ cup freshly squeezed lemon juice

¼ cup chopped fresh mint

¼ cup olive oil

Salt and freshly ground black pepper to taste

1 (3-pound) butterflied boneless leg of lamb (see method in Chapter 9)

3–4 (12-inch) metal skewers

½ head romaine lettuce, rinsed and dried

Middle Eastern Lamb Salad

Yield: 6–8 servings | Active time: 25 minutes | Start to finish: 1¼ hours

1. Place bulgur in a large mixing bowl. Stir in boiling water, cover the bowl, and allow bulgur to stand for 1 hour. Add beans, tomatoes, parsley, scallions, lemon juice, mint, olive oil, salt, and pepper to bulgur, and mix well. Refrigerate salad, tightly covered.

2. Prepare a hot grill according to the instructions given in Chapter 1. Preheat the oven to 375°F.

3. Sprinkle lamb with salt and pepper. Spear lamb lengthwise through the thickest part of the meat with the skewers to keep it level. Sear lamb on hot grill, uncovered, for 4 minutes per side.

4. Remove lamb from the grill, and place in a broiler pan. Roast lamb for 15–20 minutes, or until it registers 125°F for medium-rare on an instant-read thermometer. Remove lamb from the oven, and cover it loosely with foil. Allow lamb to rest for 10 minutes, then carve into slices across the grain.

5. To serve, line a platter or individual plates with lettuce leaves, and mound bulgur salad on top of lettuce. Top salad with lamb slices, and serve immediately.

Note: The lamb can be seared up to 4 hours in advance and kept at room temperature. The bulgur salad can be made up to 1 day in advance and refrigerated, tightly covered.

Spanish Pork and Orange Salad

Yield: 4–6 servings | Active time: 20 minutes | Start to finish: 1 hour

1. Prepare a medium-hot grill according to the instructions given in Chapter 1. Rinse pork and pat dry with paper towels.

2. Combine paprika, mustard, thyme, garlic, salt, and cayenne in a small bowl. Rub pork with vegetable oil, and then rub in spice mixture.

3. Prepare oranges; first cut away peel and the white pith below it. Then, to separate orange segments from internal membranes, slice down to the core on either side of each segment, holding fruit over a bowl to catch the juice. Set segments aside as you go.

4. Combine orange juice from bowl, vinegar, cumin, coriander, salt, and pepper in a jar with a tight-fitting lid, and shake well. Add olive oil, and shake well again.

5. Grill pork, turning it occasionally with tongs, for a total of 15–20 minutes, or until an instant-read meat thermometer registers 150°F. Transfer pork to a platter, and allow it to rest for 5 minutes.

6. Combine oranges, spinach, and onion in a large mixing bowl. Toss salad with ⅓ cup dressing. Mound mixture onto a serving platter or individual plates, and top with pork slices. Serve immediately, passing extra dressing separately.

Note: The dressing can be made up to 1 day in advance and refrigerated, tightly covered. Bring to room temperature before using.

2 (¾-pound) pork tenderloins, trimmed of excess fat and silver skin (see method in Chapter 9)

2 tablespoons smoked Spanish paprika

2 teaspoons dry mustard

1 tablespoon fresh thyme or 1 teaspoon dried

3 garlic cloves, peeled and crushed

Salt and cayenne to taste

2 tablespoons vegetable oil

3 navel oranges

3 tablespoons sherry vinegar

2 teaspoons ground cumin

1 teaspoon ground coriander

Freshly ground black pepper to taste

½ cup extra-virgin olive oil

1 pound fresh baby spinach, washed and stemmed if necessary

½ small red onion, peeled and thinly sliced

Chapter 12

Combination Cooking

This chapter is not one you will find in many cookbooks on grilling; it is the result of literally decades of experimentation as I have tried to push the limits of what can be cooked on a grill and how to give food the best flavor. All of the recipes in this chapter start on the grill; they are then finished in a conventional oven. Some recipes are roasted in a relatively cool oven to complete cooking, while others begin by being seared or smoked on the grill and are then braised to that wonderful term—fork tender.

Timing Rolled Roasts

Roasts cook more evenly if they are boned and rolled rather than left on the bone. While bones help retain moisture, the meat next to bones does not cook at the same rate since the bones act as insulation against the air carrying the heat. When tied, the string should be firm enough to hold the meat together in a neat cylinder, but should not be so tight as to be pressing into the flesh so that the exterior of the roast is bumpy. When the tissue is compressed at the points where the strings are tied, those portions of meat will cook at a slower rate, so the interior will not be evenly cooked.

Here is a chart of the general temperatures to which meats are roasted:

Roasting Temperature for Meats	
MEAT	**DESIRED INTERNAL TEMPERATURE**
Beef and Lamb	120°F—Rare 125°F–130°F—Medium-Rare 135°F—Medium
Pork	145°F–150°F
Veal	150°F–155°F

While most cookbooks calculate roasting times in an equation of minutes per pound, I have a different method. I roast meats by the circumference. A 3-pound boneless pork loin can be short and squat or it can be long and thin.

The easiest way to determine the circumference of a roast is with a tape measure. Stand the roast on its end, and place the tape measure snugly around what would be the waistline. Here is a chart to help you judge when to start taking the temperature of different roasts:

Roasting Times for Meats			
CIRCUMFERENCE	BEEF/LAMB (125°F)	VEAL (150°F)	PORK (150°F)
9 inches	30–35 min.	50–55 min.	55–60 min.
10 inches	35–45 min.	55–65 min.	60–70 min.
11 inches	45–50 min.	65–70 min.	75–85 min.
12 inches	55–60 min.	70–75 min.	85–95 min.
13 inches	60–65 min.	75–85 min.	95–105 min.
14 inches	70–75 min.	85–95 min.	105–115 min.
15 inches	75–80 min.	95–110 min.	115–125 min.
16 inches	80–90 min.	110–115 min.	125–130 min.

These are total times for boneless roasts, with the initial searing taking place on the grill, and then the meat roasted in a 350°F oven for the remainder of the cooking time.

2 cups apple or cherry
wood chips

1 (3- or 4-rib) standing rib
roast, about 6 pounds

Salt and freshly ground
black pepper to taste

1 tablespoon fresh thyme
or 1 teaspoon dried

1 tablespoon chopped
fresh rosemary or 1
teaspoon dried

"Sunday Dinner" Midwest Smoked Prime Rib of Beef

Yield: 4–6 servings | Active time: 20 minutes | Start to finish: 2 hours

1. Prepare a medium-hot grill according to the instructions given in Chapter 1. If using a charcoal grill, soak wood chips in water for 30 minutes. If using a gas grill, create a packet for wood chips as described in Chapter 1.

2. Rinse beef and pat dry with paper towels. Use kitchen twine to tie roast at both ends, parallel to the bones, if your butcher has not done so. Combine salt, pepper, thyme, and rosemary in a small bowl, and rub mixture over all surfaces of beef.

3. Preheat the oven to 350°F. Place wood chips on the grill. Sear beef on the grill for 40 minutes, covered, turning with tongs to sear all sides. Remove beef from the grill and place in a roasting pan.

4. Roast beef, uncovered, for 45–60 minutes, or until the temperature registers 125°F on an instant-read thermometer for medium-rare. The roasting time will depend on the thickness of the meat. Remove beef from the oven and place it on a platter loosely covered with aluminum foil. Allow beef to rest for 15 minutes to allow juices to be reabsorbed into meat. Then carve, and serve immediately.

Note: The roast can be seared up to 3 hours in advance of roasting it; keep it at room temperature, lightly covered.

"Sunday Dinner" Midwest Smoked Prime Rib of Beef

Leg of Lamb with Garlic, Rosemary, and Lemon
Yield: 6–8 servings | Active time: 20 minutes | Start to finish: 1½ hours

½ leg of lamb, boned, rolled, and tied, to yield 3 pounds meat

1 cup mesquite chips

10 garlic cloves, peeled

Zest of 1 lemon, cut into thin strips

3 sprigs fresh rosemary, stems removed

Salt and freshly ground black pepper to taste

1 tablespoon kosher salt

1 teaspoon freshly ground black pepper

½ cup beef stock

1. Allow meat to reach room temperature and cut deep slits into any thick portions with a paring knife.

2. Prepare a hot grill according to the instructions given in Chapter 1. If using a charcoal grill, soak mesquite chips in water for 30 minutes. If using a gas grill, create a packet for wood chips as described in Chapter 1.

3. Combine garlic, lemon zest, and rosemary leaves in a food processor fitted with a steel blade and chop finely using on-and-off pulsing. Scrape mixture into a small bowl, and stir in salt and pepper. Stuff garlic mixture into all the crevices that were formed when the meat was boned, as well as into the slits. Rub some of mixture all over exterior of roast.

4. Preheat the oven to 350°F. Place mesquite chips on the grill. Sear lamb for a total of 10 minutes, covered, turning with tongs to sear all sides. Remove lamb from the grill and place in a roasting pan.

5. Roast lamb, uncovered, for 45–60 minutes, or until the temperature registers 125°F on an instant-read thermometer. The roasting time will depend on the thickness of the roll; consult the chart at the beginning of this chapter. Remove lamb from the oven and place it on a platter loosely covered with aluminum foil. Allow lamb to rest for 15 minutes to allow juices to be reabsorbed into meat.

6. Pour grease out of the roasting pan and pour in stock. Place the pan over medium-high heat and stir often to dislodge any brown bits clinging to the bottom of the pan. Carve the meat into slices, adding any juices to the pan, and pass sauce separately.

Note: The roast can be seared up to 3 hours in advance of roasting it; keep it at room temperature, lightly covered.

2 cups hickory or apple wood chips

1 (3-pound) boneless center-cut pork loin roast

5 garlic cloves, peeled and minced, divided

2 tablespoons dried sage

1 tablespoon dried thyme

½ teaspoon ground allspice

Salt and freshly ground black pepper to taste

3 large tomatoes, cut in half

1 large onion, cut in half

1 Granny Smith apple, peeled, cored, and quartered

½ cup granulated sugar

½ cup cider vinegar

¼ cup golden raisins

2 tablespoons grated fresh ginger

¼ teaspoon cayenne

Pork Loin with Smoked Apple Chutney

Yield: 6–8 servings | Active time: 25 minutes | Start to finish: 1¾ hours

1. Prepare a hot grill according to the instructions given in Chapter 1. If using a charcoal grill, soak hickory or apple wood chips in water for 30 minutes. If using a gas grill, create a packet for wood chips as described in Chapter 1.

2. Rinse pork and pat dry with paper towels. Combine 3 garlic cloves, sage, thyme, allspice, salt, and pepper in a small bowl. Rub mixture into surfaces of pork.

3. Preheat the oven to 350°F. Place wood chips on the grill. Sear pork for a total of 10 minutes, covered, turning with tongs to sear all sides. Remove pork from the grill and place in a roasting pan.

4. Roast pork, uncovered, for 45–60 minutes, or until the temperature registers 145°F on an instant-read thermometer. The roasting time will depend on the thickness of the meat; consult the chart at the beginning of this chapter.

5. While pork roasts, prepare chutney. Cover the grill with a small-holed fish grill and place tomatoes, onion, and apple on the grill. Cover the grill with a lid and smoke vegetables and apple for 10 minutes. Remove vegetables and apple from the grill. Peel, core, and seed tomatoes. Peel and finely dice onion and apple. Place them in a large saucepan and add remaining garlic, sugar, vinegar, raisins, ginger, and cayenne.

6. Bring chutney to a boil over medium heat. Simmer, uncovered, for 30 minutes, or until thick, stirring occasionally.

7. Remove pork from the oven and place it on a platter loosely covered with aluminum foil. Allow pork to rest for 15 minutes to allow juices to be reabsorbed into meat. Then slice thinly against the grain. Serve immediately, and pass chutney separately.

Note: The roast can be seared up to 3 hours in advance of roasting it; keep it at room temperature, lightly covered.

Aromatic Roast Chicken

Yield: 4 servings | Active time: 15 minutes | Start to finish: 2 hours

1. Prepare a medium-hot grill according to the instructions given in Chapter 1. If using a charcoal grill, soak wood chips in water for 30 minutes. If using a gas grill, create a packet for wood chips as described in Chapter 1.

2. Rinse chicken, and pat dry with paper towels. Place 2 sprigs each of parsley and rosemary, 3 garlic cloves, and orange quarters in cavity of chicken. Sprinkle salt and pepper inside cavity, and close cavity with skewers.

3. Chop remaining parsley, rosemary, and garlic, and mix with butter. Season to taste with salt and pepper. Gently stuff mixture under skin of breast meat. Rub skin with salt and pepper. Truss chicken, if desired.

4. Preheat the oven to 350°F. Place wood chips on the grill. Sear chicken for a total of 15 minutes, covered, turning with tongs to brown all sides. Remove chicken from the grill, and place in a roasting pan, breast side up.

5. Add onion, carrot, celery, and ½ cup chicken stock to the roasting pan. Cook an additional 1–1¼ hours, or until the juices run clear and the temperature of the dark meat registers 180°F on an instant-read thermometer. Remove chicken from the oven, and allow it to rest for 10 minutes, lightly covered.

6. Spoon all grease out of the pan, and add remaining chicken stock to the pan. Stir over medium-high heat until liquid is reduced to a syrupy consistency. Strain sauce into a sauce boat, and add to it any liquid that accumulates on the platter when chicken is carved. Carve chicken, and serve immediately.

VARIATION: *Tarragon can be substituted for the rosemary and parsley, and white wine can be used instead of chicken stock.*

Note: The chicken can be prepared for searing and roasting up to 6 hours in advance and refrigerated, tightly covered.

Ingredients

1 cup mesquite, hickory, or apple wood chips

1 (3½–4-pound) whole chicken, giblets removed

4 sprigs fresh parsley, divided

4 sprigs fresh rosemary, divided

6 garlic cloves, peeled, divided

1 orange, quartered

Salt and freshly ground black pepper to taste

4 tablespoons (½ stick) unsalted butter, softened

1 small onion, peeled and roughly chopped

1 carrot, peeled and thickly sliced

1 celery rib, rinsed, trimmed, and roughly chopped

1½ cups chicken stock, divided

1 cup mesquite chips

6 (1-pound) lamb shanks

Salt and freshly ground
  black pepper to taste

⅓ cup olive oil

2 medium onions, peeled
  and diced

2 celery ribs, rinsed,
  trimmed, and diced

2 carrots, peeled, trimmed,
  and sliced

4 garlic cloves, peeled and
  minced

2 tablespoons chopped
  fresh parsley

1 tablespoon chopped
  fresh rosemary or 1
  teaspoon dried

1 tablespoon chopped
  fresh oregano or 1
  teaspoon dried

2 teaspoons fresh thyme or
  ½ teaspoon dried

2 tablespoons tomato
  paste

1½ cups Barolo, or other
  dry red wine

1 cup beef stock

1 tablespoon cornstarch

2 tablespoons cold water

Braised Lamb Shanks

Yield: 6 servings | Active time: 20 minutes | Start to finish: 3 hours

1. Prepare a medium-hot grill according to the instructions given in Chapter 1. If using a charcoal grill, soak mesquite chips in water for 30 minutes. If using a gas grill, create a packet for wood chips as described in Chapter 1.

2. Wipe lamb shanks well with a damp cloth and remove any fat. Season with salt and pepper, and set aside.

3. While grill heats, heat oil in a Dutch oven over medium-high heat. Add onions, celery, carrots, and garlic, and cook, stirring frequently, for 3 minutes, or until onions are translucent.

4. Preheat the oven to 350°F. Place mesquite chips on the grill. Sear lamb shanks for a total of 15 minutes, covered, turning shanks with tongs to sear all sides.

5. Transfer shanks to the Dutch oven, and add parsley, rosemary, oregano, thyme, tomato paste, wine, and stock. Bring to a boil on top of the stove, then transfer to the oven, and bake for 1½–2 hours, or until fork tender.

6. Remove shanks to a warm platter and tip the Dutch oven to spoon off as much grease as possible. Cook sauce over medium heat until reduced by ½ . Mix cornstarch and water in a small cup, and add to sauce. Simmer for 3 minutes or until slightly thickened. Season sauce to taste with salt and pepper, then pour sauce over shanks, and serve immediately.

Note: The shanks can be prepared up to 3 days in advance and refrigerated. If cooked in advance, remove the layer of grease, which will have hardened on the top. Reheat, covered, in a 350°F oven for 25–35 minutes, or until hot.

Braised Lamb Shanks

2 cups hickory or mesquite chips

1 (3–4-pound) beef brisket

2 garlic cloves, peeled and crushed

Salt and freshly ground black pepper to taste

2 cups beef stock

1 cup My Favorite Barbecue Sauce (recipe on page 16) or commercial barbecue sauce, heated

Smoked Beef Brisket with Barbecue Sauce

Yield: 8–10 servings | Active time: 20 minutes | Start to finish: 3½ hours

1. Prepare a medium-hot grill according to the instructions given in Chapter 1. If using a charcoal grill, soak hickory or mesquite chips in water for 30 minutes. If using a gas grill, create a packet for wood chips as described in Chapter 1.

2. Rinse brisket and pat dry with paper towels. Rub brisket with garlic, and season to taste with salt and pepper.

3. Preheat the oven to 350°F. Place wood chips on the grill. Sear brisket, covered, for a total of 20 minutes, turning with tongs after 10 minutes.

4. Transfer brisket to a roasting pan, and add stock. Bring to a boil on top of the stove, then transfer to the oven, and bake for 2–2½ hours, covered, or until fork tender.

5. Remove brisket to a warm platter and tip the roasting pan to spoon off as much grease as possible. Slice brisket against the grain into thin slices. Spoon some pan juices over meat, and pass barbecue sauce separately.

VARIATION: *You can also use this recipe for a boneless pork shoulder; the cooking time will be reduced to 1½–2 hours.*

Note: The brisket can be prepared up to 2 days in advance and refrigerated. If cooked in advance, remove the layer of grease, which will have hardened on the top. Reheat, covered, in a 350°F oven for 25–35 minutes, or until hot.

Chapter 13

Pizzas

Cooking thin-crust pizzas on the grill is now all the rage, and they can be topped with myriad ingredients. While authentic in some parts of Italy, it was American restaurant chefs who popularized the grilled pizza in this country, many of which are on the menus of restaurants in the Italian sections of large Midwestern cities like Chicago and Detroit.

The key to a successful grilled pizza is that it must be small; it is impossible to flip a large round on the grill, and it is essential to grill both sides of the dough. I usually make pizzas in two batches, and cut up the first batch to allow diners to start munching while the second batch cooks. If your grill is large enough to accommodate all four circles at once, go ahead and cook them simultaneously.

For an easy alternative to making pizza dough, in almost all cities you can now purchase ready-to-bake balls of pizza dough in the refrigerated dairy case. With a few balls of pizza dough handy, any pizza can be on the table in less time than it takes to have one delivered!

Basic Pizza Dough and Procedure

Yield: 4 (8-inch) pizzas | Active time: 15 minutes | Start to finish: 50 minutes, including 30 minutes for rising

3 cups all-purpose flour, plus extra for working dough

1 package active dry or fresh yeast

1 teaspoon salt

1 tablespoon honey

2 tablespoons olive oil

¾ cup water

1. Place flour and yeast in a mixing bowl or the bowl of an electric mixer fitted with a dough hook. Add salt, honey, olive oil, and water. Mix well until the dough forms a soft ball.

2. Transfer dough to a lightly floured surface and knead for 5 minutes or until smooth. Place dough in a greased deep mixing bowl and allow dough to rest, covered with a clean dry towel, for 30 minutes.

3. Divide dough into 4 equal parts, and roll each piece into a smooth, tight ball. Place balls on a flat dish, covered with a damp towel, and refrigerate until grilling time. (This can be done up to 6 hours in advance, but dough should be removed from the refrigerator 1 hour before grilling to reach room temperature.)

4. Lightly flour a work surface, and using the fleshy part of your fingertips, flatten each dough ball into a circle, approximately 6 inches in diameter, leaving outer edge thicker than center. Dust dough on both sides with flour. Lift dough from the work surface and gently stretch the edges, working clockwise, to form a dough circles that is ¼ inch thick. Sprinkle additional flour on pizza paddles or baking sheets, and place pizza circles on top of flour. Lightly rub a long sheet of plastic wrap with flour, then invert loosely over pizza rounds and let them stand to puff slightly while preparing the grill, 10 to 20 minutes.

VARIATIONS: *Feel free to add a few tablespoons of chopped fresh herbs such as basil, oregano, or parsley to the basic pizza dough.*

---

1 recipe Basic Pizza Dough or purchased pizza dough

8 ripe plum tomatoes, rinsed, cored, seeded, and chopped

¼ cup extra-virgin olive oil, divided

Salt and freshly ground black pepper to taste

½ pound whole-milk mozzarella cheese, thinly sliced

½ cup firmly packed fresh basil leaves

¼ cup freshly grated Parmesan cheese

2 (10-inch) aluminum pie tins

Pizza Margherita

Yield: 4 servings | Active time: 20 minutes | Start to finish: 30 minutes

1. Prepare a medium-hot grill according to the instructions given in Chapter 1. Shape pizza dough into 4 individual ¼-inch-thick rounds as described above in the recipe for Basic Pizza Dough.

2. Place tomatoes in a sieve set over a mixing bowl to drain. Brush dough rounds with olive oil, and sprinkle with salt and pepper. Gently flip 2 dough rounds onto the grill, oiled side down. Grill, uncovered, for 1½–2 minutes, or until grill marks form; burst bubbles that may appear on the surface with a long-handled meat fork. Brush tops with olive oil, and invert pizzas onto a baking sheet with the grilled side up.

3. Cover crusts with mozzarella and then tomatoes, stopping ½ inch from the edge. Scatter basil and Parmesan over the top. Season to taste with salt and pepper, and drizzle with more olive oil.

4. Return pizzas to the grill, and cover with pie tins. Grill, covered, for 1½–2 minutes, or until browned and cheese has melted. Serve immediately, and repeat with remaining 2 pizza rounds.

VARIATION: *While it would not be authentic, either fresh oregano or fresh chopped rosemary can be substituted for the basil.*

Prosciutto Pizza

Yield: 4 servings | Active time: 15 minutes | Start to finish: 35 minutes

1. Prepare a medium-hot grill according to the instructions given in Chapter 1. Shape pizza dough into 4 individual ¼-inch-thick rounds as described above in the recipe for Basic Pizza Dough.

2. Heat ¼ cup olive oil in a large skillet over medium-high heat. Add red bell peppers and cook, stirring frequently, for 5 minutes or until peppers are soft. Mix remaining ¼ cup oil with crushed red pepper, and set aside. Combine mozzarella and fontina cheeses, and set aside.

3. Brush dough rounds with seasoned olive oil, and sprinkle with salt and pepper. Gently flip 2 dough rounds onto the grill, oiled side down. Grill, uncovered, for 1½–2 minutes, or until grill marks form; burst bubbles that may appear on the surface with a long-handled meat fork. Brush tops with olive oil, and invert pizzas onto a baking sheet with the grilled side up.

4. Spread mixed cheeses on top, reserving 1 cup cheese, stopping ½ inch from the edge. Sprinkle with basil, and top with tomatoes, prosciutto, red peppers, and scallions. Dot with goat cheese, and finish by sprinkling with reserved cheese.

5. Return pizzas to the grill, and cover with pie tins. Grill, covered, for 1½–2 minutes, or until browned and cheese has melted. Serve immediately, and repeat with remaining 2 pizza rounds.

1 recipe Basic Pizza Dough or purchased pizza dough

½ cup olive oil, divided

2 red bell peppers, seeds and ribs removed, and thinly sliced

1 tablespoon crushed red pepper flakes

¾ pound fresh whole-milk mozzarella, grated

¼ pound fontina cheese, grated

Salt and freshly ground black pepper to taste

½ cup chopped fresh basil

4 ripe plum tomatoes, rinsed, cored, seeded, and thinly sliced

6 ounces prosciutto, cut into fine julienne strips

4 scallions, white parts and 2 inches of green tops, rinsed, trimmed, and thinly sliced

4 ounces fresh goat cheese, crumbled

2 (10-inch) aluminum pie tins

1 recipe Basic Pizza Dough or purchased pizza dough

¼ pound smoked bacon

¼ cup extra-virgin olive oil

Salt and freshly ground pepper to taste

3 cups grated cheddar cheese

4 ripe plum tomatoes, rinsed, cored, seeded, and thinly sliced

1 cup sliced mushrooms

2 (10-inch) aluminum pie tins

Bacon, Tomato, Mushroom, and Cheddar Pizza

Yield: 4 servings | Active time: 15 minutes | Start to finish: 35 minutes

1. Prepare a medium-hot grill according to the instructions given in Chapter 1. Shape pizza dough into 4 individual ¼-inch-thick rounds as described above in the recipe for Basic Pizza Dough.

2. Place bacon slices in a heavy skillet, and cook over medium-high heat, turning pieces as necessary, until bacon is crisp. Remove bacon with tongs, and drain on paper towels. When cool, crumble bacon, and set aside.

3. Brush dough rounds with olive oil, and sprinkle with salt and pepper. Gently flip 2 dough rounds onto the grill, oiled-side down. Grill, uncovered, for 1½–2 minutes, or until grill marks form; burst bubbles that may appear on the surface with a long-handled meat fork. Brush tops with olive oil, and invert pizzas onto a baking sheet with the grilled side up.

4. Cover crusts with cheddar, then tomatoes and mushrooms, stopping ½ inch from the edge. Scatter bacon over the top. Season to taste with salt and pepper.

5. Return pizzas to the grill, and cover with pie tins. Grill, covered, for 1½–2 minutes, or until browned and cheese has melted. Serve immediately, and repeat with remaining 2 pizza rounds.

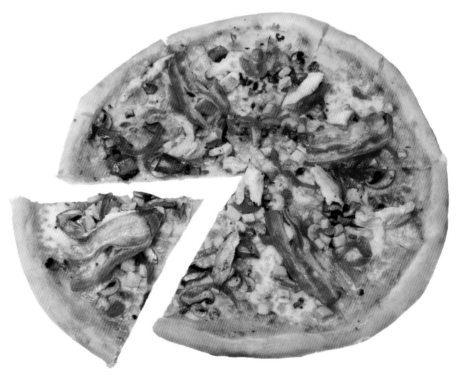

Bacon, Tomato, Mushroom, and Cheddar Pizza

Provençal Vegetable Pizza

Yield: 4 servings | Active time: 20 minutes | Start to finish: 35 minutes

1. Prepare a medium-hot grill according to the instructions given in Chapter 1. Shape pizza dough into 4 individual ¼-inch-thick rounds as described above in the recipe for Basic Pizza Dough.

2. Brush squash, eggplant, and pepper slices with olive oil, and sprinkle with salt and pepper. Grill squash and eggplant for 2 minutes per side, covered, or until tender. Grill pepper slices for 5 minutes per side, covered, or until tender. When cool enough to handle, slice peppers into thin strips. Combine tapenade, oregano, parsley, and thyme in a small bowl, and stir well. Set aside.

3. Brush dough rounds with olive oil, and sprinkle with salt and pepper. Gently flip 2 dough rounds onto the grill, oiled side down. Grill, uncovered, for 1½–2 minutes, or until grill marks form; burst bubbles that may appear on the surface with a long-handled meat fork. Brush tops with olive oil, and invert pizzas onto a baking sheet with the grilled side up.

4. Spread crusts with tapenade mixture, stopping ½ inch from the edge. Divide a quarter of vegetables on top of tapenade, and then sprinkle with ½ cup cheese.

5. Return pizzas to the grill, and cover with pie tins. Grill, covered, for 1½–2 minutes, or until browned and cheese has melted. Serve immediately, and repeat with remaining 2 pizza rounds.

Note: The vegetables can be grilled up to 1 day in advance and refrigerated, tightly covered. Allow them to reach room temperature before using.

1 recipe Basic Pizza Dough or purchased pizza dough

2 medium yellow squash, trimmed and cut into ¼-inch slices

2 Italian eggplants, trimmed and cut into ¼-inch slices

1 red bell pepper, seeds and ribs removed, and quartered lengthwise

½ cup extra-virgin olive oil, divided

Salt and freshly ground black pepper to taste

¾ cup black olive tapenade, homemade or purchased

3 tablespoons chopped fresh oregano or 1 tablespoon dried

2 tablespoons chopped fresh parsley

1 tablespoon fresh thyme or 1 teaspoon dried

2 cups grated Gruyère cheese

2 (10-inch) aluminum pie tins

4 ripe plum tomatoes, rinsed, cored, seeded, and diced

½ cup chopped pitted kalamata olives

¼ cup chopped red onion

4 tablespoons olive oil, divided

2 tablespoons chopped fresh oregano or 2 teaspoons dried

Salt and freshly ground black pepper to taste

4 (8-inch) whole-wheat pita breads

½ cup crumbled feta cheese

2 (10-inch) aluminum pie tins

Greek-Style Pita Pizzas

Yield: 4 servings | Active time: 10 minutes | Start to finish: 35 minutes

1. Prepare a medium-hot grill according to the instructions given in Chapter 1. Combine tomatoes, olives, onion, 2 tablespoons olive oil, oregano, salt, and pepper in a mixing bowl. Mix well.

2. Brush pita bread with olive oil, and sprinkle with salt and pepper. Gently flip 2 pita breads onto the grill, oiled side down. Grill, uncovered, for 1½–2 minutes, or until grill marks form. Brush tops with olive oil, and invert pitas onto a baking sheet with the grilled side up.

3. Cover crusts with vegetable mixture, stopping ½ inch from the edge. Scatter feta over the top. Season to taste with salt and pepper.

4. Return pizzas to the grill, and cover with pie tins. Grill, covered, for 1½–2 minutes, or until browned and cheese has melted. Serve immediately.

Greek-Style Pita Pizzas

Chapter 14

Vegetables

It is only in recent decades that Americans have come to appreciate the wonderful flavors and textures that result from grilling vegetables. Cooking vegetables over high heat evaporates some of the high water content, and, therefore, intensifies the natural, sweet flavor and natural sugar in vegetables.

Grilling accentuates vegetables' natural sugars.

4–6 ears fresh corn

Kitchen twine

3 tablespoons unsalted butter, melted

Salt and freshly ground black pepper to taste

Grilled Corn

Yield: 4–6 servings | Active time: 10 minutes | Start to finish: 35 minutes

1. Prepare a medium-hot grill according to the instructions given in Chapter 1.

2. Break stem end off corn, and discard all but 1 layer of husks. Pull back remaining husks, and pull off as much corn silk as possible. Draw husks back over kernels, and tie husks with kitchen twine. Soak corn in cold water to cover for 10 minutes.

3. Grill corn, uncovered if using a charcoal grill, for a total of 8–10 minutes, turning it with tongs every 1½–2 minutes. Corn is done when husks are charred and outline of kernels is visible.

4. Remove corn from the grill, and when cool enough to handle, remove and discard husks and any remaining corn silks. To serve, brush corn with melted butter, and season with salt and pepper to taste. Serve immediately.

Grilled Corn

Grilled Asparagus

Yield: 4–6 servings | Active time: 10 minutes | Start to finish: 30 minutes

10 (8-inch) bamboo skewers

2 pounds medium asparagus

3 tablespoons olive oil

Salt and freshly ground black pepper to taste

1. Soak bamboo skewers in warm water to cover, and prepare a medium-hot grill according to the instructions given in Chapter 1.

2. Break off woody ends from asparagus, soak asparagus in water to cover for 10 minutes, and rub the tips to dislodge any lingering grit.

3. Divide asparagus into groups, and thread them horizontally with 2 skewers per bunch into loose groups; do not push them together too tightly. Brush asparagus with oil, and sprinkle with salt and pepper.

4. Grill asparagus, covered, for 3–4 minutes per side, turning bunches with tongs. Serve immediately.

Rosemary Potatoes

Yield: 4–6 servings | Active time: 20 minutes | Start to finish: 1 hour

8–12 (8-inch) bamboo skewers

1½ pounds baby potatoes, no more than 2 inches in diameter, scrubbed and halved

Salt and freshly ground black pepper to taste

⅓ cup olive oil, divided

3 tablespoons finely chopped fresh rosemary

1. Soak bamboo skewers in warm water to cover, and prepare a medium-hot grill according to the instructions given in Chapter 1.

2. Place potatoes in a saucepan, and cover with cold water. Salt water, and bring potatoes to a boil over high heat. Reduce the heat to medium-high, and boil potatoes for 10–12 minutes, or until just tender. Drain potatoes, and toss them with ¼ cup olive oil, rosemary, salt, and pepper.

3. Thread potatoes onto 2 parallel skewers. Grill potatoes, uncovered if using a charcoal grill, for a total of 4–5 minutes, turning them with tongs occasionally, or until grill marks appear. Remove skewers from the grill, and drizzle with remaining olive oil. Serve immediately.

VARIATION: *In place of rosemary, try fresh oregano or basil in this recipe. You can add a few crushed garlic cloves to the oil, too.*

4 medium ripe tomatoes

2 tablespoons extra-virgin olive oil

1 garlic clove, peeled and pressed through a garlic press

1 teaspoon dried oregano

1 teaspoon dried thyme

Salt and freshly ground black pepper

⅔ cup Greek Feta Sauce (recipe on page 19)

Herbed Tomatoes with Greek Feta Sauce
Yield: 4 servings | Active time: 10 minutes | Start to finish: 35 minutes

1. Prepare a medium-hot grill according to the instructions given in Chapter 1. Cut tomatoes in half, and squeeze gently to remove seeds.

2. Combine oil, garlic, oregano, thyme, salt, and pepper in a small bowl, and stir well. Brush mixture on both sides of tomato halves.

3. Grill tomatoes skin side up, uncovered if using a charcoal grill, for 3–4 minutes, or until grill marks show. Turn tomatoes gently with tongs and grill for an additional 2–3 minutes, or until hot. Serve immediately, passing Greek Feta Sauce separately.

Herbed Tomatoes with Greek Feta Sauce

Sesame Radicchio

Yield: 4–6 servings | Active time: 20 minutes | Start to finish: 45 minutes

1. Prepare a medium-hot grill according to the instructions given in Chapter 1.

2. Trim root ends from radicchio, and cut each head into quarters, leaving core attached. Brush radicchio and scallions with 2 tablespoons sesame oil, and sprinkle with salt and pepper. Set aside.

3. Combine vinegar, soy sauce, mirin or sherry, garlic, ginger, and pepper in a jar with a tight-fitting lid, and shake well. Add remaining sesame oil and vegetable oil, and shake well again. Set aside.

4. Grill radicchio for 3 minutes per side, covered, turning wedges with tongs. Grill scallions for a total of 4 minutes, turning them once. Remove vegetables from the grill.

5. Cut core from radicchio wedges, and cut each wedge crosswise into ½-inch strips. Cut scallions into thirds. Transfer vegetables to a mixing bowl, and toss with dressing. Sprinkle with sesame seeds, and serve immediately.

Note: The dressing can be prepared up to 1 day in advance and refrigerated, tightly covered. Allow it to reach room temperature before using.

3 (4-inch) heads radicchio

12 scallions, white parts and 1 inch of green tops, rinsed and trimmed

¼ cup Asian sesame oil,* divided

Salt and freshly ground black pepper to taste

¼ cup rice wine vinegar

2 tablespoons soy sauce

1 tablespoon mirin* or sherry

2 garlic cloves, peeled and minced

2 teaspoons grated fresh ginger

¼ cup vegetable oil

3 tablespoons sesame seeds, toasted

* Available in the Asian aisle of most supermarkets and in specialty markets.

Herbed Zucchini

Yield: 4–6 servings | Active time: 15 minutes | Start to finish: 35 minutes

1. Prepare a medium-hot grill according to the instructions given in Chapter 1.

2. Cut zucchini in half lengthwise. Cut a thin slice off the curved side of each half with a paring knife so that zucchini sit securely on the counter. Combine oil, oregano, parsley, thyme, garlic, salt, and pepper in a blender. Puree until smooth, and scrape mixture into a small bowl.

3. Brush both sides of zucchini slices with oil, and grill for 4–5 minutes per side, uncovered if using a charcoal grill, turning slices with tongs. Serve immediately or at room temperature.

Note: The zucchini and oil mixture can be prepared up to 6 hours in advance and refrigerated, tightly covered.

4–6 small zucchini, rinsed and trimmed

⅓ cup extra-virgin olive oil

2 tablespoons fresh oregano or 2 teaspoons dried

¼ cup firmly packed fresh parsley leaves

2 teaspoons fresh thyme or ½ teaspoon dried

1 garlic clove, peeled

Salt and freshly ground black pepper to taste

8–12 (8-inch) bamboo
skewers

¼ cup olive oil

3 garlic cloves, peeled and
minced

1 red onion, peeled

2 orange or yellow bell
peppers, seeds and ribs
removed, and halved

1 Italian eggplant

2 small zucchini, trimmed

2 portobello mushroom
caps, stemmed and wiped
with a damp paper towel

Salt and freshly ground
black pepper to taste

Mixed Vegetable Kebabs

Yield: 4–6 servings | Active time: 20 minutes | Start to finish: 45 minutes

1. Soak bamboo skewers in warm water to cover, and prepare a medium-hot grill according to the instructions given in Chapter 1.

2. Mix garlic with oil, and set aside. Cut onion in half horizontally, and then cut halves into 8 wedges each. Cut bell peppers into 1½-inch squares. Cut eggplant into 1½-inch cubes. Cut zucchini into 1½-inch segments. Cut mushroom caps into eighths.

3. Rub all vegetables with garlic oil, and sprinkle with salt and pepper.

4. Thread vegetables alternately onto 2 parallel skewers. Grill kebabs, covered, giving them quarter turns every 2½–3 minutes, for a total of 10–12 minutes, or until vegetables are tender. Remove kebabs from the grill, and serve immediately.

Note: The kebabs can be prepared for grilling up to 6 hours in advance and kept at room temperature.

Chapter 15

Non-Grilled Side Dishes

While there are recipes for vegetable and other side dishes in this book that are cooked on the grill, there are many times that the grill is reserved for the entree, and the supporting players are created in the kitchen. It is in this chapter that you will find those recipes.

In the Midwest, side dishes are primarily simple and homey, and because the climate rarely reaches the high heat and humidity associated with other regions, it is common to serve hot side dishes even in the summer months.

Baked Macaroni and Cheese

1 pound elbow macaroni or
other short pasta

4 tablespoons (½ stick)
unsalted butter

¼ cup all-purpose flour

1 tablespoon paprika

¼ teaspoon cayenne

1 cup chicken stock

2 cups whole milk

4 cups (1 pound) grated
sharp cheddar cheese,
divided

1 tablespoon Dijon
mustard

Salt and freshly ground
black pepper to taste

Baked Macaroni and Cheese

Yield: 6–8 servings | Active time: 15 minutes | Start to finish: 45 minutes

1. Preheat the oven to 400°F, and grease a 10 x 14-inch baking pan.

2. Bring a large pot of salted water to a boil. Add macaroni, and cook according to package directions until al dente. Drain, and place in a mixing bowl.

3. Heat butter in a 2-quart saucepan over low heat. Stir in flour, paprika, and cayenne, and stir constantly for 2 minutes. Whisk in stock, and bring to a boil over medium-high heat, whisking constantly. Reduce the heat to low, and simmer 2 minutes. Stir in milk and 3½ cups grated cheese, and stir until cheese is melted. Stir in mustard, and season to taste with salt and pepper.

4. Stir sauce into macaroni, and transfer mixture to the prepared pan. Cover the pan with foil, and bake for 10 minutes. Uncover the pan, sprinkle with remaining ½ cup cheese, and bake for an additional 15–20 minutes, or until bubbly. Allow to sit for 5 minutes, then serve.

Note: The macaroni can be prepared for baking up to 2 days in advance and refrigerated, tightly covered. Add 10 minutes to the covered baking time if chilled.

7 tablespoons unsalted
butter, divided

5 large eggs

1½ cups half-and-half

¼ cup all-purpose flour

3 cups fresh corn kernels
(about 5 or 6 ears)

4 scallions, white parts and
2 inches of green tops,
rinsed, trimmed, and
chopped

½ red bell pepper, seeds
and ribs removed, and
finely chopped

2 tablespoons chopped
fresh parsley

2 teaspoons fresh thyme
leaves or ½ teaspoon
dried

Salt and freshly ground
black pepper to taste

Corn Pudding

Yield: 6–8 servings | Active time: 20 minutes | Start to finish: 1 hour

1. Preheat the oven to 350°F, and grease a 2-quart soufflé dish or ovenproof casserole with 1 tablespoon butter. Melt remaining butter, and set aside.

2. Whisk eggs with butter, half-and-half, and flour. Stir in corn, scallions, red pepper, parsley, thyme, salt, and pepper.

3. Pour mixture into the prepared dish, and place pudding in a roasting pan. Pour boiling water into the roasting pan to halfway up the sides of the dish. Bake for 45 minutes, or until top of pudding is brown and a knife inserted in the center comes out clean. Allow to sit for 5 minutes before serving.

Note: The pudding can be prepared for baking up to 1 day in advance and refrigerated, tightly covered. Increase the baking time by 10 minutes if the pudding is baked chilled.

Deviled Eggs

Yield: 18 pieces | Active time: 15 minutes | Start to finish: 45 minutes

9 large eggs

⅓ cup mayonnaise

2 teaspoons Dijon mustard

¼ cup finely chopped sweet pickles

¼ cup finely chopped celery

Salt and freshly ground black pepper to taste

Paprika

1. Place eggs in a saucepan, and cover with cold water to 2 inches above the tops of eggs. Bring to a boil over high heat, uncovered. Boil for 1 minute, cover the pan, and remove the pan from the heat. Allow eggs to sit for 15 minutes, covered. Drain eggs, and fill pan with cold running water for 3 minutes to stop the cooking action. Allow eggs to sit in cold water for 10 minutes, then peel eggs and halve them lengthwise.

2. Carefully remove yolks from eggs, and place them in a food processor fitted with a steel blade. Add mayonnaise and mustard, and process until light and fluffy. This can also be done by hand using a fork to mash mixture. Stir in pickles and celery, and season to taste with salt and pepper.

3. Pipe mixture into egg whites with a pastry bag fitted with a large fluted tip. Sprinkle with paprika, and serve immediately.

VARIATION: *Instead of the pickles, use 3 tablespoons chopped fresh dill in the egg filling.*

Note: The deviled eggs can be assembled 3 hours in advance and refrigerated, tightly covered. Do not sprinkle them with paprika until just before serving.

Deviled Eggs

6 tablespoons (¾ stick) unsalted butter, divided

1 cup yellow cornmeal

1 cup all-purpose flour

2 tablespoons granulated sugar

1½ teaspoons baking powder

½ teaspoon baking soda

¼ teaspoon salt

2 large eggs

¾ cups buttermilk

½ cup creamed corn

Cornbread

Yield: 6–8 servings | Active time: 10 minutes | Start to finish: 30 minutes

1. Preheat the oven to 425° F. Grease a 9 x 9-inch square pan generously with 1 tablespoon butter. Melt remaining butter, and set aside.

2. Whisk together cornmeal, flour, sugar, baking powder, baking soda, and salt in a large mixing bowl. Whisk together eggs, buttermilk, creamed corn, and butter in a small bowl. Add buttermilk mixture to cornmeal mixture, and stir batter until just blended.

3. Heat the greased pan in the oven for 3 minutes, or until it is very hot. Remove the pan from the oven, and spread batter in it evenly. Bake cornbread in the middle of the oven for 15 minutes, or until top is pale golden and the sides begin to pull away from the edges of the pan.

4. Allow cornbread to cool for 5 minutes, then turn it out onto a rack. Cut into pieces, and serve hot or at room temperature.

Note: The cornbread is best eaten within a few hours of baking.

Cornbread

Buttermilk Biscuits

Yield: 20 (2-inch) biscuits | Active time: 10 minutes | Start to finish: 30 minutes

1½ cups cake flour (not self-rising)

½ cup all-purpose flour

1 tablespoon baking powder

½ teaspoon salt

½ teaspoon baking soda

6 tablespoons vegetable shortening

⅔ cup buttermilk

3 tablespoons unsalted butter, melted

1. Preheat oven to 425°F, and lightly grease a baking sheet.

2. Sift cake flour, all-purpose flour, baking powder, salt, and baking soda into a large mixing bowl. Cut in vegetable shortening using a pastry blender, two knives, or your fingertips until mixture resembles coarse meal. Add buttermilk, and stir with a fork until just combined.

3. Transfer mixture to a lightly floured surface, and knead 10 times with the heel of your hand to bring the dough together. Pat dough into a round that is ½ inch thick.

4. Cut dough into 2-inch circles and place them 1 inch apart on the prepared baking sheet. Brush tops with melted butter. Gather scraps and pat into a circle again to cut out more biscuits. Repeat until all dough is used.

5. Bake for 18–20 minutes, or until cooked through and golden brown. Serve immediately.

VARIATIONS: *For cheese biscuits, add ½ cup grated cheddar cheese to the dough. For a sweet biscuit, combine ½ cup firmly packed dark brown sugar, ½ cup finely chopped toasted pecans, and ½ teaspoon ground cinnamon in a mixing bowl, and pat mixture onto the top of unbaked biscuits.*

Note: The biscuits can be cut out up to 1 hour in advance. Do not bake them until just prior to serving.

Red Cabbage Slaw

Yield: 6–8 servings | Active time: 25 minutes | Start to finish: 3½ hours, including 2 hours to marinate and 1 hour to chill

1 (1½-pound) red cabbage, cored and shredded

2 carrots, peeled and coarsely grated

½ red onion, peeled and thinly sliced

2 tablespoons grated fresh ginger

¾ cup cider vinegar

3 tablespoons honey

3 tablespoons vegetable oil

Salt and freshly ground black pepper to taste

½ cup golden raisins

3 scallions, trimmed and thinly sliced

1. Place cabbage, carrots, and red onion in a vegetable steamer set over boiling water. Steam for 5 minutes, drain, and place vegetables in a mixing bowl.

2. Combine ginger, vinegar, honey, oil, and salt and pepper in a jar with a tight-fitting lid. Shake well, and pour dressing over steamed vegetables. Marinate at room temperature for 2 hours, stirring occasionally.

3. Plump raisins in boiling water for 15 minutes. Drain and add to salad. Place salad in a colander set over another mixing bowl. Drain vegetables, pressing with the back of a spoon to extract as much liquid as possible.

4. Place juice in a small saucepan and boil it over medium-high heat until only ½ cup remains. Stir reduced dressing back into the salad along with the scallions. Chill salad for at least 1 hour before serving.

Note: The salad can be made up to 1 day in advance and refrigerated, tightly covered.

½ cup sugar

½ cup cider vinegar

⅓ cup vegetable oil

1 tablespoon celery seeds

1 tablespoon dry mustard

Salt and freshly ground black pepper to taste

1 (2-pound) head green cabbage, cored and shredded

1 small red onion, peeled and thinly sliced

1 green pepper, seeds and ribs removed, and thinly sliced

1 red bell pepper, seeds and ribs removed, and thinly sliced

Celery Seed Slaw

Yield: 6–8 servings | Active time: 20 minutes | Start to finish: 6¼ hours, including 5 hours to marinate and chill

1. Combine sugar, vinegar, and oil in a small saucepan, and bring to a boil over medium heat, stirring occasionally. Reduce the heat to low and stir in celery seeds, mustard, salt, and pepper. Simmer for 2 minutes, stirring occasionally.

2. Combine cabbage, onion, green pepper, and red pepper in a large mixing bowl. Toss dressing with salad. Allow slaw to sit at room temperature for 2 hours, tossing it occasionally. Refrigerate slaw for 3–4 hours. Drain well before serving.

Note: The slaw can be made 1 day in advance and refrigerated, tightly covered with plastic wrap.

3 cucumbers, peeled, halved, lengthwise, seeded, and thinly sliced

½ large sweet onion, such as Vidalia or Bermuda, peeled and thinly sliced

1 cup rice wine vinegar

3 tablespoons chopped fresh dill

2 tablespoons granulated sugar

Salt and freshly ground white pepper to taste

Dilled Cucumbers

Yield: 6–8 servings | Active time: 10 minutes | Start to finish: 2 hours 10 minutes, including 2 hours for marinating

1. Combine cucumbers and onion in a heavy, resealable plastic bag. Combine vinegar, dill, sugar, salt, and pepper in a jar with a tight-fitting lid. Shake well to dissolve sugar.

2. Add cucumbers, and marinate for at least 2 hours, refrigerated, turning the bag occasionally. Drain marinade from salad. Serve chilled.

Note: The salad can be made up to 2 days in advance and refrigerated, tightly covered.

Garden Potato Salad

Yield: 6–8 servings | Active time: 20 minutes | Start to finish: 4 hours, including 3 hours to chill potatoes

2 pounds small redskin potatoes, scrubbed
1 cucumber, peeled
1 green bell pepper, seeds and ribs removed
1 small red onion, peeled
3 celery ribs, rinsed and trimmed
½ cup mayonnaise
3 tablespoons white wine vinegar
Salt and freshly ground black pepper to taste

1. Place potatoes in a large saucepan of cold salted water. Bring potatoes to a boil over high heat, reduce the heat to medium, and boil potatoes for 10–20 minutes, or until they are tender when pierced with the tip of a paring knife. Drain potatoes and chill well. Cut potatoes into 1-inch cubes, and place them in a large mixing bowl.

2. Cut cucumber in half lengthwise and scrape out the seeds with a teaspoon. Slice cucumber into thin arcs, and add to potatoes. Cut green pepper into 1-inch sections and slice each section into thin strips. Add to the mixing bowl. Cut onion in half through the root end, and cut each half into thirds. Cut into thin slices and add to the mixing bowl. Cut each celery rib in half lengthwise and thinly slice the celery. Add to the mixing bowl.

3. Toss potato salad with mayonnaise and vinegar, and season to taste with salt and pepper. Serve well chilled.

Note: The salad can be made 1 day in advance and refrigerated, tightly covered.

Hash-Brown Potato Salad with Bacon and Onion

Yield: 6–8 servings | Active time: 20 minutes | Start to finish: 45 minutes

1½ pounds boiling potatoes, quartered lengthwise and cut crosswise into 1-inch slices
¼ pound bacon, cut into ½-inch slices
2 tablespoons vegetable oil
1 tablespoon mustard seeds
1 tablespoon chopped fresh rosemary or 1 teaspoon dried
3 tablespoons cider vinegar, divided
½ red onion, peeled and finely chopped
1 celery rib, rinsed, trimmed, and thinly sliced
⅓ cup mayonnaise, or to taste
2 tablespoons chopped fresh parsley
Salt and freshly ground black pepper to taste

1. Steam potatoes in a steamer set over boiling water, covered, for 6–8 minutes, or until barely tender. Remove potatoes from the steamer, and set aside.

2. Cook bacon in a large skillet over medium-high heat until crisp. Remove bacon from the pan with a slotted spoon, drain on paper towels, and set aside. Discard all but 2 tablespoons of bacon fat. Add oil to the skillet, heat over medium heat, and fry mustard seeds, partially covered, for 10 seconds, or until they stop popping.

3. Add potatoes and rosemary to the skillet, and cook, turning potatoes carefully, for 10 minutes. Add 2 tablespoons vinegar and cook the potatoes, turning carefully, for 5 minutes, or until crusty and golden.

4. Transfer potatoes to a large bowl, and cool. Add onion and celery to potatoes. Thin mayonnaise with remaining 1 tablespoon vinegar, and add it to salad along with bacon, parsley, salt, and pepper. Toss salad gently, and serve salad at room temperature.

Note: The salad can be made 1 day in advance and refrigerated, tightly covered. Allow the salad to come back to room temperature before serving.

Wild Rice Salad with Dried Cranberries

Yield: 6–8 servings | Active time: 20 minutes | Start to finish: 1 hour

1 pound wild rice

Salt and freshly ground black pepper to taste

¼ cup balsamic vinegar

1 tablespoon Dijon mustard

1 large shallot, peeled and minced

½ cup olive oil

1½ cups chopped pecans, toasted in a 350°F oven for 5–7 minutes

1 cup dried cranberries

¼ cup chopped fresh parsley

1. Rinse wild rice in a sieve under cold running water. Place it in a saucepan and add cold water to cover by 3 inches. Season water with salt and pepper, and bring to a boil over medium-high heat. Reduce the heat to low and simmer rice, covered, for 45–55 minutes, or until tender and fully puffed. Rinse rice under cold water, and place in a salad bowl.

2. While rice cooks, combine vinegar, mustard, shallot, salt, and pepper in a jar with a tight-fitting lid, and shake well. Add oil, and shake well again. Set aside.

3. Add pecans, dried cranberries, and parsley to rice, and toss with dressing. Serve immediately.

Note: The salad can be served at room temperature or chilled, and it can be refrigerated for up to 2 days, tightly covered.

Baked Beans

Yield: 6–8 servings | Active time: 15 minutes | Start to finish: 5½ hours

1 pound dried navy beans

¼ pound bacon, cut into ½-inch pieces

1 large onion, peeled and diced

2 garlic cloves, peeled and minced

6 cups water

1 cup ketchup

½ cup firmly packed dark brown sugar

¼ cup apple cider vinegar

2 tablespoons dry mustard

Salt and freshly ground black pepper to taste

1. Place beans in a saucepan and cover with water. Bring to a boil over high heat, and boil 1 minute. Turn off the stove, cover the pan, and allow beans to soak, covered, for 1 hour. Drain, and set aside. (Alternately, cover beans with cold water and allow them to sit at room temperature for a minimum of 6 hours or overnight.)

2. Preheat the oven to 350°F.

3. Place bacon in a Dutch oven, and cook over medium-high heat until crisp. Remove bacon from the pan with a slotted spoon, and set aside. Discard all but 2 tablespoons of bacon grease from the pan. Add onion and garlic to the pan, and cook, stirring frequently, for 3 minutes, or until onion is translucent.

4. Add beans and bacon to the pan, and add water, ketchup, sugar, vinegar, mustard, salt, and pepper. Stir well, and bring to a boil over medium heat, stirring occasionally.

5. Transfer the pan to the oven, and bake for 3½–4 hours, stirring occasionally, or until beans are soft and liquid is thick. Serve hot.

Note: The beans can be baked up to 3 days in advance and refrigerated, tightly covered. Reheat them in a 300°F oven for 40 minutes, covered, or until hot.

Midwest Onion Pie

Yield: 6–8 servings | Active time: 20 minutes | Start to finish: 1¼ hours

1. Heat butter in a large saucepan over low heat. Add onions, toss to coat, and cover the pan. Cook over low heat for 10 minutes, stirring occasionally. Uncover the pan, raise the heat to medium, and stir in salt, pepper, and sugar. Cook for 30–40 minutes, stirring frequently, or until onions have turned dark brown. If onions stick to the pan, stir to incorporate the browned juices into the onions. Set aside to cool.

2. Preheat the oven to 350°F. Roll puff pastry ⅛-inch thick. Place pastry on a baking sheet, and bake for 15 minutes.

3. Whisk egg yolks and cream, and stir in cooled onions. Spread mixture on top of the pastry. Sprinkle with cheese, and bake for 25 minutes. Cut into 6–8 squares or rectangles. Serve immediately.

Note: The pastry base and filling can be made 1 day in advance. Refrigerate the filling, and add 5 minutes to the baking time.

4 tablespoons (½ stick) unsalted butter

2 large sweet onions, such as Bermuda, or Vidalia, peeled and thinly sliced

Salt and freshly ground black pepper to taste

2 teaspoons granulated sugar

¼ pound frozen puff pastry, thawed

2 large egg yolks

¼ cup heavy cream

½ cup grated Swiss or Gruyère cheese

Garden Vegetable Custard

Yield: 6–8 servings | Active time: 25 minutes | Start to finish: 1½ hours

1. Place eggplant in a colander and sprinkle liberally with salt. Place a plate on top of eggplant cubes, and weight the plate with cans. Place the colander in a sink or on a plate and allow eggplant to drain for 30 minutes. Rinse eggplant cubes and pat dry on paper towels.

2. Heat olive oil in a large skillet over medium-high heat. Add onions and garlic and cook, stirring frequently, for 3 minutes, or until onions are translucent. Add eggplant, red pepper, zucchini, tomatoes, basil, and thyme to the pan. Cook for 5 minutes, stirring frequently.

3. Reduce the heat to low, and cook vegetables for 20 minutes, covered, or until they are soft and the liquid has almost evaporated. Season to taste with salt and pepper, and let cool 10 minutes.

4. Preheat the oven to 350°F, and grease a 9 x 13-inch baking dish. Whisk eggs with sour cream, salt, and pepper. Stir eggs into vegetable mixture and pour it into the prepared pan. Bake custard for 45 minutes, or until eggs are set and the top is lightly browned. Serve hot, at room temperature, or chilled.

Note: The custard can be made 1 day in advance and refrigerated, tightly covered, if it is to be served chilled. Do not reheat it.

1 (1-pound) eggplant, rinsed, trimmed, and cut into ½-inch dice

Salt and freshly ground black pepper to taste

¼ cup olive oil

3 onions, peeled and diced

2 garlic cloves, peeled and minced

1 red bell pepper, seeds and ribs removed, cut into ½-inch dice

2 small zucchini, rinsed, trimmed, and cut into ½-inch dice

4 plum tomatoes, rinsed, cored, seeded, and cut into ½-inch dice

2 tablespoons chopped fresh basil or 1 teaspoon dried

1 tablespoon fresh thyme leaves or ½ teaspoon dried

6 large eggs

¼ cup sour cream

Chapter 16

Grilled Desserts

The title of this chapter is not an oxymoron, nor is it just variations on toasted marshmallows—although there is a recipe for S'mores. What you will find when cooking these recipes is that the grill is a natural way to glean the most luscious flavor from fruit; fruit desserts comprise the majority of these recipes. It should come as no surprise that heating enhances all of fruit's natural sweetness, as well as creating a softer texture.

¾ cup dark rum

8 tablespoons (1 stick) unsalted butter

¼ cup firmly packed dark brown sugar

½ teaspoon ground cinnamon

¼ teaspoon pure vanilla extract

1 ripe pineapple

3–4 cups vanilla ice cream

½ cup chopped toasted walnuts (optional)

Rum-Glazed Pineapple

Yield: 6–8 servings | Active time: 15 minutes | Start to finish: 30 minutes

1. Prepare a medium-hot grill according to the instructions given in Chapter 1.

2. Combine rum, butter, sugar, cinnamon, and vanilla in a small saucepan. Cook over medium heat, stirring frequently, for 15 minutes, or until thickened. Set aside.

3. While sauce simmers, cut rind off pineapple, and cut in half vertically. Cut out and discard core, and cut pineapple into ⅓-inch slices. Set aside.

4. Grill pineapple slices for 1½–2 minutes per side, uncovered if using a charcoal grill, or until browned, brushing them with sauce frequently. To serve, place pineapple slices on plates and top with ice cream and additional sauce. Serve immediately, garnished with nuts, if using.

Note: The sauce can be made up to 2 days in advance and refrigerated, tightly covered. Reheat it over low heat or in a microwave oven before using.

Grilled Banana Splits

Yield: 4–6 servings | Active time: 10 minutes | Start to finish: 30 minutes

1. Prepare a medium-hot grill according to the instructions given in Chapter 1.

2. Slice bananas in half lengthwise and crosswise so each banana is cut into quarters. Mix sugar and cinnamon, and rub mixture into cut sides of bananas.

3. Grill bananas, cut side down, for 2 minutes, or until grill marks appear. Turn bananas and grill an additional 2–3 minutes, or until bananas are soft.

4. To serve, remove skin from bananas, and place 4 pieces in the bottom of each serving bowl. Top bananas with 2 scoops ice cream, ¼ cup chocolate sauce, and 1–2 tablespoons chopped nuts. Top with whipped cream and cherries, if using. Serve immediately.

4–6 ripe bananas, unpeeled

2 tablespoons firmly packed light brown sugar

1 teaspoon ground cinnamon

8–12 small scoops vanilla ice cream

1½ cup Chocolate Sauce (recipe follows), heated

½ cup coarsely chopped toasted walnuts

Sweetened whipped cream (optional)

4–6 maraschino cherries or strawberries (optional)

Grilled Banana Splits

5 ounces good-quality bittersweet chocolate

½ cup heavy cream

3 tablespoons unsweetened cocoa powder

1 tablespoon rum

¼ teaspoon pure vanilla extract

Pinch of salt

Chocolate Sauce

Yield: 1½ cups | Active time: 10 minutes | Start to finish: 15 minutes

1. Chop chocolate into pieces no larger than a lima bean, and set aside.

2. Pour cream into a 1-quart saucepan, and place over medium heat. Whisk in cocoa powder, rum, vanilla, and salt. Bring to a boil, whisking frequently, until mixture is smooth.

3. When cream begins to boil, remove pan from the heat. Add chocolate, cover pan, and allow to sit for 5 minutes; whisk well until sauce is smooth. If lumps remain, place sauce over low heat and continue to whisk until smooth.

4. Scrape mixture into a container, and refrigerate for up to 1 week or freeze for up to 3 months. To serve, microwave sauce on MEDIUM (50% power) for 30-second intervals or until liquid and warm, stirring well between microwave times.

4–6 navel oranges

1 pint fresh raspberries, rinsed

2 tablespoons granulated sugar

2 tablespoons Grand Marnier, triple sec, or another orange-flavored liqueur

1 pint vanilla ice cream or vanilla frozen yogurt

Grilled Oranges with Raspberry Sauce

Yield: 4–6 servings | Active time: 10 minutes | Start to finish: 30 minutes

1. Prepare a medium-hot grill according to the instructions given in Chapter 1.

2. Grate 2 teaspoons zest off oranges, and then peel oranges. Cut each into 4 slices horizontally. Combine raspberries, sugar, Grand Marnier, and orange zest in a small mixing bowl. Mash fruit gently, and set aside.

3. Grill orange slices for 1½–2 minutes per side, uncovered if using a charcoal grill, or until browned. To serve, arrange orange slices on the bottom of bowls, and top with ice cream and raspberry sauce. Serve immediately.

Note: The raspberry sauce can be made up to 6 hours in advance and kept at room temperature.

Nouvelle Peach Melba

Yield: 4–6 servings | Active time: 20 minutes | Start to finish: 30 minutes

4–6 ripe peaches, unpeeled

¾ cup granulated sugar, divided

⅔ cup freshly squeezed orange juice

2 tablespoons freshly squeezed lemon juice, divided

¼ teaspoon pure vanilla extract

1 pint fresh raspberries, rinsed, or 1 (8-ounce) package frozen dry-packed raspberries, thawed

2 tablespoons Chambord or other berry-flavored liqueur

1 pint vanilla ice cream

1. Prepare a medium-hot grill according to the instructions given in Chapter 1.

2. Cut peaches in half and discard stones. Place peaches in a 9 x 13-inch pan, cut side up.

3. Combine ⅔ cup sugar, orange juice, 1 tablespoon lemon juice, and vanilla in a small saucepan, and stir well. Bring to a boil over medium-high heat, and boil for 2 minutes, stirring occasionally. Pour syrup over peaches, and set aside.

4. Combine raspberries, remaining sugar, remaining lemon juice, and Chambord in a food processor fitted with a steel blade or in a blender. Puree until smooth, and strain mixture. Refrigerate until ready to use.

5. Drain peaches, and grill skin-side up for 4 minutes, uncovered if using a charcoal grill, then turn peaches with tongs and grill skin-side down for an additional 3–4 minutes, or until peaches are tender. To serve, place 2 peach halves in the bottom of each bowl, and top with ice cream and raspberry sauce. Serve immediately.

Note: Raspberry sauce can be made up to 1 day in advance and refrigerated, tightly covered.

Candy Bar Quesadillas

Yield: 4–6 servings | Active time: 10 minutes | Start to finish: 30 minutes

8 (8-inch) flour tortillas

Vegetable oil spray

1 (8-ounce) package cream cheese, softened

4 (2-ounce) candy bars, such as Snickers, Almond Joy, Milky Way, or any chocolate bar, each cut into 15 thin slices

4 tablespoons confectioners' sugar

1. Prepare a medium-hot grill according to the instructions given in Chapter 1.

2. Wrap tortillas in plastic wrap and microwave on HIGH (100% power) for 20 seconds, or until pliable. Spray 4 tortillas with vegetable oil spray, and place them sprayed side down on a cookie sheet. Spread tortillas with ¼ of cream cheese to within ½-inch of the edge. Top cheese with candy bar slices.

3. Top with remaining 4 tortillas, and press with the palm of your hand or a spatula to close them firmly. Spray tops of quesadillas with vegetable oil spray.

4. Grill quesadillas, covered, for 2 minutes. Turn gently with a wide spatula and grill for an additional 2 minutes, or until brown and crisp. Remove quesadillas from the grill, and sprinkle with confectioners' sugar. Allow quesadillas to sit for 2 minutes, then cut each into 6 sections and serve immediately.

Note: The quesadillas can be prepared 1 day in advance of grilling them. Refrigerate them, tightly covered with plastic wrap, and bring them back to room temperature before grilling.

Ultimately Messy S'mores

24 graham crackers or sweet whole-wheat crackers, such as Carr's wheatmeal biscuits

1½ (3-ounce) dark chocolate bars or any flavored chocolate bar, broken into ½-inch pieces

12 large marshmallows

Ultimately Messy S'mores

Yield: 4–6 servings | Active time: 10 minutes | Start to finish: 35 minutes

1. Prepare a medium-hot grill according to the instructions given in Chapter 1. Cut 12 (8-inch) squares of aluminum foil.

2. Place 1 cracker in the center of each foil sheet, and top with chocolate. Toast marshmallows over the grill on a long-handled fork, and place on top of chocolate. Top marshmallows with remaining crackers, and enclose sandwiches in foil.

3. Grill foil packets for 2 minutes, or until chocolate is melted and gooey. Unwrap, and serve immediately.

1 pint fresh strawberries, rinsed, stemmed, and sliced

½ pint fresh raspberries, rinsed

½ pint fresh blueberries, rinsed

2 tablespoons crème de cassis or Chambord

1 teaspoon grated lemon zest

4–6 (¾-inch) slices pound cake, homemade or purchased

1 pint strawberry ice cream, or your favorite flavor

Toasted Cake with Berry Sauce

Yield: 4–6 servings | Active time: 15 minutes | Start to finish: 30 minutes

1. Prepare a medium-hot grill according to the instructions given in Chapter 1.

2. Place ½ of strawberries in a food processor fitted with a steel blade or in a blender; puree until smooth. Combine puree, remaining strawberries, raspberries, blueberries, crème de cassis, and lemon zest in a mixing bowl, and stir well. Refrigerate, tightly covered, until ready to use.

3. Grill cake slices, uncovered if using a charcoal grill, for 1 minute per side or until grill marks appear. To serve, place cake slices on plates and top with ice cream and fruit sauce. Serve immediately.

Note: Fruit sauce can be made up to 1 day in advance and chilled, tightly covered.

Cream Cheese Frosting

Yield: Enough for 1 (3-layer) cake | Active time: 10 minutes | Start to finish: 10 minutes

1. Combine cream cheese and butter in a large mixing bowl, and beat at medium speed with an electric mixer until light and fluffy.

2. Reduce the speed to low, and beat in the confectioners' sugar and vanilla. Beat for 2 minutes.

VARIATION: *If you want a crunchier frosting, add 1 cup chopped walnuts which have been previously toasted in a 350˚F oven for 5–7 minutes.*

Note: The frosting can be prepared up to 6 hours in advance and kept at room temperature with a sheet of plastic wrap pushed into the surface.

3 (8-ounce) packages cream cheese, softened

6 tablespoons (¾ stick) unsalted butter, softened

6 cups (1½ pounds) confectioners' sugar

2 teaspoons pure vanilla extract

Strawberry Shortcake

Yield: 6 servings | Active time: 15 minutes | Start to finish: 40 minutes, including 10 minutes for cooling

1. Preheat the oven to 375˚F and grease 2 baking sheets with 1 tablespoon butter. Combine flour, sugar, cream of tartar, baking soda, and salt in a medium mixing bowl. Melt 3 tablespoons butter, and set aside. Cut remaining butter into ¼-inch cubes.

2. Cut cubed butter into flour mixture using a pastry blender, 2 knives, or your fingertips until mixture resembles coarse meal. Add 1 cup cream, and blend until just blended.

3. Scrape dough onto a floured surface, and knead lightly. Roll dough to a thickness of ¾ inch. Cut out 6 (4-inch) rounds and place them on the baking sheet. Brush rounds with melted butter. Cut out 6 (2½-inch) rounds and place them on top of larger rounds. Brush tops with butter.

4. Bake for 15–17 minutes or until shortcakes are golden brown. Cool for at least 10 minutes on a wire rack.

5. While shortcakes bake, rinse strawberries, discard green caps, and slice. Toss strawberries with crème de cassis. Set aside. Just prior to serving, whip remaining cream with confectioners' sugar until stiff peaks form.

6. To serve, mound strawberries on larger round, and top with whipped cream and smaller round. Serve immediately.

VARIATION: *Any berry can be substituted for the strawberries, as can peeled peach slices.*

Note: The shortcakes can be baked up to 6 hours in advance and kept at room temperature.

½ pound (2 sticks) unsalted butter, divided

3 cups all-purpose flour

⅓ cup granulated sugar

1 tablespoon cream of tartar

2¼ teaspoons baking soda

¼ teaspoon salt

2 cups heavy cream, divided

1 quart strawberries

⅓ cup crème de cassis or Chambord

⅓ cup confectioners' sugar

1½ cups graham cracker crumbs, or any cookie crumb, such as vanilla wafers or gingersnaps

5 tablespoons unsalted butter, melted

2 cups granulated sugar, divided

4 (8-ounce) packages cream cheese, softened

3 tablespoons all-purpose flour

4 large eggs

2 large egg yolks

2 teaspoons grated lemon zest

½ teaspoon pure vanilla extract

Pinch of salt

Midwest Cheesecake

Yield: 10–12 servings | Active time: 40 minutes | Start to finish: 8 hours, including 7 hours for chilling

1. Preheat the oven to 500°F.

2. Combine crumbs, butter, and ⅓ cup sugar in a mixing bowl, and stir well. Pat mixture into bottom and 1 inch up the sides of a 12-inch springform pan. Set aside.

3. Combine remaining sugar, cream cheese, and flour in a large mixing bowl, and beat at medium speed with an electric mixer until smooth. Add eggs and egg yolks, 1 at a time, beating well between each addition and scraping the sides of the bowl as necessary. Beat in lemon zest, vanilla, and salt. Scrape mixture into the pan on top of crust.

4. Bake in the center of the oven for 15 minutes. Reduce the oven temperature to 225°F and continue to bake cheesecake for an additional 1 hour. Turn off oven, and allow cheesecake to sit in the oven for an additional 30 minutes.

5. Cool cake in the pan on a rack, and then refrigerate until cold. Run a knife around the sides of the pan to release cake, and then remove sides of pan. Allow cheesecake to sit at room temperature for 30 minutes before serving.

Note: Cheesecake lasts forever! You can refrigerate this cake for up to 1 week; keep it tightly covered with plastic wrap.

Midwest Cheesecake

Oatmeal Raisin Cookies

Oatmeal Raisin Cookies

Yield: 24 cookies | Active time: 15 minutes | Start to finish: 30 minutes

1. Preheat the oven to 375°F, and grease 2 baking sheets with 1 tablespoon butter.

2. Sift together flour, cinnamon, baking soda, and salt. Place remaining butter, granulated sugar, and brown sugar in a large mixing bowl. Beat with an electric mixer on low speed to combine, then raise the speed to high and beat for 2 minutes, or until light and fluffy. Add eggs and vanilla and beat for 2 minutes more. Reduce the speed to low and add flour mixture until just blended. Stir in oats, raisins, and walnuts.

3. Drop batter by rounded tablespoons onto the baking sheets, spacing them 2 inches apart. Bake for 12 minutes for chewy cookies or 15 minutes for crisp cookies. Move cookies with a spatula to a cooling rack, and cool completely.

Note: The cookies can be stored refrigerated for up to 1 week, tightly covered.

7 tablespoons unsalted butter, divided

1 cup all-purpose flour

1 teaspoon ground cinnamon

½ teaspoon baking soda

Pinch of salt

½ cup granulated sugar

½ cup firmly packed dark brown sugar

2 large eggs, at room temperature

1 teaspoon pure vanilla extract

1¼ cups quick-cooking or old-fashioned oats (not instant)

1 cup raisins

1 cup chopped walnuts, toasted in a 350°F oven for 5 minutes

Appendix A

Metric Conversion Tables

The scientifically precise calculations needed for baking are not necessary when cooking conventionally. The tables in this appendix are designed for general cooking. If making conversions for baking, grab your calculator and compute the exact figure.

Converting Ounces to Grams

The numbers in the following table are approximate. To reach the exact amount of grams, multiply the number of ounces by 28.35.

OUNCES	GRAMS
1 ounce	30 grams
2 ounces	60 grams
3 ounces	85 grams
4 ounces	115 grams
5 ounces	140 grams
6 ounces	180 grams
7 ounces	200 grams
8 ounces	225 grams
9 ounces	250 grams
10 ounces	285 grams
11 ounces	300 grams
12 ounces	340 grams
13 ounces	370 grams
14 ounces	400 grams
15 ounces	425 grams
16 ounces	450 grams

Converting Quarts to Liters

The numbers in the following table are approximate. To reach the exact amount of liters, multiply the number of quarts by 0.95.

QUARTS	LITERS
1 cup (¼ quart)	¼ liter
1 pint (½ quart)	½ liter
1 quart	1 liter
2 quarts	2 liters
2½ quarts	2½ liters
3 quarts	2¾ liters
4 quarts	3¾ liters
5 quarts	4¾ liters
6 quarts	5½ liters
7 quarts	6½ liters
8 quarts	7½ liters

Converting Pounds to Grams and Kilograms

The numbers in the following table are approximate. To reach the exact amount of grams, multiply the number of pounds by 453.6.

POUNDS	GRAMS; KILOGRAMS
1 pound	450 grams
1½ pounds	675 grams
2 pounds	900 grams
2½ pounds	1,125 grams; 1¼ kilograms
3 pounds	1,350 grams
3½ pounds	1,500 grams; 1½ kilograms
4 pounds	1,800 grams
4½ pounds	2 kilograms
5 pounds	2¼ kilograms
5½ pounds	2½ kilograms
6 pounds	2¾ kilograms
6½ pounds	3 kilograms
7 pounds	3¼ kilograms
7½ pounds	3½ kilograms
8 pounds	3¾ kilograms

Converting Fahrenheit to Celsius

The numbers in the following table are approximate. To reach the exact temperature, subtract 32 from the Fahrenheit reading, multiply the number by 5, and then divide by 9.

DEGREES FAHRENHEIT	DEGREES CELSIUS
170°F	77°C
180°F	82°C
190°F	88°C
200°F	95°C
225°F	110°C
250°F	120°C
300°F	150°C
325°F	165°C
350°F	180°C
375°F	190°C
400°F	205°C
425°F	220°C
450°F	230°C
475°F	245°C
500°F	260°C

Converting Inches to Centimeters

The numbers in the following table are approximate. To reach the exact number of centimeters, multiply the number of inches by 2.54.

INCHES	CENTIMETERS
½ inch	1.5 centimeters
1 inch	2.5 centimeters
2 inches	5 centimeters
3 inches	8 centimeters
4 inches	10 centimeters
5 inches	13 centimeters
6 inches	15 centimeters
7 inches	18 centimeters
8 inches	20 centimeters
9 inches	23 centimeters
10 inches	25 centimeters
11 inches	28 centimeters
12 inches	30 centimeters

Appendix B

Measurement Tables

Table of Weights and Measures of Common Ingredients		
FOOD	QUANTITY	YIELD
Apples	1 pound	2½ to 3 cups sliced
Avocados	1 pound	1 cup mashed fruit
Bananas	1 medium	1 cup sliced
Bell Peppers	1 pound	3 to 4 cups sliced
Blueberries	1 pound	3⅓ cups
Butter	¼ pound (1 stick)	8 tablespoons
Cabbage	1 pound	4 cups packed shredded
Carrots	1 pound	3 cups diced or sliced
Chocolate, morsels	12 ounces	2 cups
Chocolate, bulk	1 ounce	3 tablespoons grated
Cocoa powder	1 ounce	¼ cup
Coconut, flaked	7 ounces	2½ cups
Cream	½ pt = 1 cup	2 cups whipped
Cream cheese	8 ounces	1 cup
Flour	1 pound	4 cups
Lemons	1 medium	3 tablespoons juice
Lemons	1 medium	2 teaspoons zest
Milk	1 quart	4 cups
Molasses	12 ounces	1½ cups
Mushrooms	1 pound	5 cups sliced
Onions	1 medium	½ cup chopped
Peaches	1 pound	2 cups sliced
Peanuts	5 ounces	1 cup
Pecans	6 ounces	1½ cups
Pineapples	1 medium	3 cups diced

Potatoes	1 pound	3 cups sliced
Raisins	1 pound	3 cups
Rice	1 pound	2 to 2½ cups raw
Spinach	1 pound	¾ cup cooked
Squash, summer	1 pound	3½ cups sliced
Strawberries	1 pint	1½ cups sliced
Sugar, brown	1 pound	2¼ cups, packed
Sugar, confectioner's	l pound	4 cups
Sugar, granulated	1 pound	2¼ cups
Tomatoes	1 pound	1½ cups pulp
Walnuts	4 ounces	1 cup

Table of Liquid Measurements	
Pinch	less than ⅛ teaspoon
3 teaspoons	1 tablespoon
2 tablespoons	1 ounce
8 tablespoons	½ cup
2 cups	1 pint
1 quart	2 pints
1 gallon	4 quarts

Index